Praise Fo

"Smart, subtle, and often very amusing...so delightful and so useful...If we all learned to listen the way Nunberg does, maybe we'd learn to speak and think better, too."—*San Jose Mercury News*

"Nunberg's approach to language is to keep a humorous detachment from disputes while lending an expert opinion."—*Chicago Tribune*

"Geoffrey Nunberg [is] a man whose ear for every insincere inflection, every fashionable prefix, every fatuous habit of media expression, is so acute that you can't help feeling a bit verbally naked in his presence."
—*Seattle Weekly*

"Although Nunberg ranges over many kinds of words, including shrewd meditations on the teenager's 'like' and the growing vogue of 'Caucasian instead of 'white'—his observations on political speech are especially valuable in revealing how words inform our understanding of issues."—*The Washington Post Book World*

"Geoffrey Nunberg has the unusual ability to ferret out those little guys skulking around in our language, using the big important words as a cover, and figure out what they're up to and what they can tell us about our political and social skills."—*San Francisco Chronicle*

"Clearly, Nunberg knows about etymology and usage and a good deal more...As a guide, Nunberg is witty, entertaining, informative and unfailingly fascinating."—*The St. Louis Post-Dispatch*

"Nunberg...is not writing for word buffs or grammatical sticklers; he is a people's linguist ... A breezy, insightful book that will provide plenty of material for good dinner-table conversation."—*Times Literary Supplement*

"Even fans who've heard (or read it) all before should find some happy surprises the second time around."—*The Boston Globe*

"Amusing. . . full of good scholarship. . . Language moves. Usually it out-runs professors, but Nunberg has a hold of the beast's tail."
—*Kansas City Star*

"I admire Nunberg's prowess at making linguistics accessible, interesting and entertaining. . . He has a knack for definitions and an amazing penchant for analyzing cultural trends. . . His social commentary is incisive and not pedantic. . . Nunberg is not only a linguist but a social historian and critic with a skewed and ironic perception of the world. . . I believe that every reader will find something to like about the book and will learn many fascinating facts. . . this book is a must for politicians and for all of those whose livelihood depends on using words properly and effectively."—*San Antonio Express-News*

"My pick for the word book of the year is *Going Nucular*, a collection of sharp essays. . . Nunberg shows how the smallest linguistic coffee bean flavors the political and cultural brew."—*Hartford Courant*

"Geoffrey Nunberg is the best kind of word nerd: He cares what words *mean*. . . . At a few pages a pop, some of *Going Nucular*'s essays stop before they've gotten every goodie out of the bag. But when gifts like a perfectly-honed attack on the term "9/11" tumble out, why grouse?"
—*Philadelphia City Paper*

"What separates Geoffrey Nunberg's *Going Nucular: Language, Politics and Culture in Confrontational Times* from a pack of similar volumes is the playful curiosity with which the author regards the English language."—*SF Weekly Magazine*

[Going Nucular]

[Going Nucular]

Language, Politics, and Culture

in Confrontational Times

Geoffrey Nunberg

PublicAffairs   New York

Book design by Mark McGarry, Texas Type & Book Works
Set in Dante

Library of Congress Cataloging-in-Publication Data
Nunberg, Geoffrey, 1945–
Going nucular: language, politics, and culture in confrontational times /
Geoffrey Nunberg.
p. cm.
ISBN 1-58648-345-5 (pbk)
1. English language—Political aspects—United States. 2. English
language—Social aspects—United States. 3. English language—United
States—Semantics. 4. English language—United States—usage. 5. Political
science—Terminology.
I. Title.
PE2809.N86 2004
420'.973—dc22
2003069022

10 9 8 7 6 5 4 3 2 1

In memory of my father, Jack,
a lover of words

[**Contents**]

WATCHING OUR LANGUAGE

[Introduction]

The great early–twentieth-century linguist Antoine Meillet once remarked that every word has its story. That's easy enough to believe when you scan the rows of books that are stashed in the language section in the back of the bookstore—the perky usage guides, the curmudgeonly diatribes about the sorry state of English, the compilations of curious foreign idioms, the Treasure-Troves of Word-Lore and Rambling Excursions Down the Highways and By-ways of Our Speech. What a bunch! I think of the way Montaigne began his essay "On Vanity," ridiculing the vast number of books on language in an earlier age: "What could come from prattle, when the stammering and loosening of the tongue could smother the world under such a frightful load of volumes? So many words for the sake of words alone!"

Speaking as a linguist, I find that dismissal a little unfair—after all, nobody is moved to derision at the thought of thousands of books about flowers, dogs, the Civil War, or any of the other topics that have alcoves consecrated to them at the back of the bookstore. But people do tend to think of a preoccupation with language as vaguely suspect. Words are a little like crossword puzzles—everyone takes a mild interest in them, but it's a little alarming to discover that someone you know is an aficionado, one of those word-buffs who sprinkle their conversation with curious etymologies and enjoy pointing out the grammatical errors on restaurant menus.

This isn't really a book for those buffs. It's short on the romance of words, and shorter still on complaints about the way the language is going to hell in a handbasket. Ultimately, it isn't chiefly about language as such—or at least, few of these pieces were written for the sake of words alone. For the most part, they take language as a jumping-off point; the object of the exercise is to see what words can tell us about other things, once we get into the habit of listening to them closely.

One thing that continues to perplex me after all these years of writing about words is just how hard it is to attend to language and how much of it slips past you, however great an effort you make to listen critically. On the basis of some rough calculations, for example, I figure that I've heard or seen the word *Caucasian* somewhere between 1,000 and 2,000 times in my life. But I never gave it a moment's thought until one day in September of 2003 when I was watching a CNN interview with a California high-school freshman who was trying to start a Caucasian club at her school for "the kids who think they're Caucasian, white, to break down their heritages and teach them their cultures." It seemed odd to me that a fifteen-year-old would know the word *Caucasian*—at least, I had the sense it wasn't a word that I would have known when I was a teenager. But when I did some counts in newspaper databases, it turned out that *Caucasian* is several times more common now than it was thirty or forty years ago.

It was only at that point that I began to realize what a weird word *Caucasian* is, particularly nowadays. Why should it be more common now, when by all rights it should be as outmoded as

Mongoloid and *Negroid* and the other old-fashioned racial terminology it came in with? What does the word do for us that *white*
doesn't, and why don't we just say "European Americans" as a
parallel to "Asian Americans," "African Americans," and the rest?
Why is it that Jews count as Caucasians nowadays (unlike fifty or
sixty years ago), whereas Arabs seem to be regarded as non-Cau-
casians, even if both groups count as white? Is this supposed to be
a question of race, or culture, or what?

Not many people who use the word *Caucasian* could give a
clear answer to those questions—not that California high-school
student, not the CNN anchor, and not me, either, though I tried
to get at some of this in one of the pieces collected here, "Caucasian Talk Circles." It reminds you that the function of words
isn't just to communicate ideas but to keep them at a certain
remove from consciousness. They're like those tinned fruitcakes
that get passed around Christmas after Christmas without anyone ever opening them or sniffing them to see if they're still
good. Sometimes the most important thing about words is what
they enable us to leave unsaid.

That's the assumption behind the game I play with myself
when I'm writing these pieces. Words usually have something to
hide—you have to shake them until the top pops off and some
revelation tumbles out, an insight into some attitude that it
would be hard to put your finger on by any other means.

The pieces collected here recount some of the ways that
words can betray our changing ideas and sensibilities. Sometimes
those shifts show up in the replacement of one word by another.
It says something about our changing sense of national purpose
that *liberty* has been losing ground to *freedom* over the past century. And it says something about our changing understanding of

economic forces that Woody Guthrie's "hard times" turns up in Bruce Springsteen's lyrics as "the economy."

On other occasions, though, people adapt an old word to a new point of view, and then go on as if nothing had happened. That can be the subtlest form of linguistic deception—as Aneurin Bevan once remarked, we have to be especially on guard against the old words that "persist when the reality behind them has changed." However much we may think of *leftist* and *liberal* as the names of immutable political poles, we don't use the words now the way we did forty years ago. Despite its deliberately archaic ring, *chastity* doesn't mean what it once did. And *protest* has changed its meaning since the 1960s—at least, no one back then would have thought of describing a demonstration in support of the administration's policies as a "pro-war protest," the way some conservatives were doing in 2003.

Or sometimes the action shows up not in cultural keywords like *leftist* or *freedom*, but the little words and particles that are particularly dear to linguists. (That's the difference between language buffs and linguists—when the former talk about the fascination of words they're thinking about something like *antimacassar* or *serendipity*; with the latter, it's more likely *and* or *the*.) What is it about the new forms of broadcast news that leads anchors to speak a tenseless form of the language, as in "The navy using the island since 1940"? Why are right-wing commentators particularly fond of connecting a series of adjectives with *and*? And why does Rush Limbaugh address his radio listeners in the plural, while NPR announcers use the singular?

I'm not one of those linguists who think that all language change is the result of ineluctable natural forces, so that we can only fold our arms and dispassionately observe the passing show.

If changes in words are often the sign of changes in values and attitudes, then we can deplore the first by way of condemning the second. I feel sure that corporations were better served when they asked their employees to come up with goals rather than missions or vision statements, and I think we do Lou Gehrig more honor by describing him as a hero rather than as a legend. And I reserve *enormity* for events of appalling horror, though that particular misgiving I usually keep to myself.

But the urge to fulminate about language can also be an impediment to understanding it. Take the use of *like* to introduce reported speech—"So she was like, 'no WAY!'" You can decry that as the sign of an endemic mindlessness and mental laxity among young people nowadays, particularly if your memories of how you talked as an adolescent are conveniently dim. But that comes at a cost of hearing what's going on with the construction. *Say* introduces a report of what someone said; *like* introduces a performance of it—a question of showing rather than telling. It's a convenient distinction to have available in colloquial speech. The only question is why English should suddenly feel the need of the device, after a thousand years of making do without it. It's hardly an answer to complain about modern adolescents' laziness and inarticulateness. In fact, the real laziness here is in the critics who pronounce about the language in the assurance that they're smarter than it is. The worst offense you can commit against language is to fail to listen to it closely.

One problem with taking language as a point of departure is that you're likely to wind up in exotic intellectual territory before you're through—you start on familiar linguistic grounds and all of a sudden you find yourself in need of some help with Islamic theology, the history of economics, Cold War politics, or the inner workings of search engines. In writing these pieces, I've relied heavily on the invaluable and (apart from here) uncredited help of a number of friends and colleagues, including Francesco Antinucci, Mark Aronoff, Khalil Barhoum, Howard Bloch, Lisa Brennan, Gordon Chang, Jessica Coope, Ayman Farahat, Linda Georgianna, Carla Hesse, Larry Horn, Arthur Knight, John Lamping, Tom Laqueur, Jonathan Lighter, Larry Masinter, Joe Pickett, Leah Price, John Rickford, Debarati Sanyal, Tony Sarmiento, Hinrich Schuetze, Annie Zaenen, and Arnold Zwicky. And I owe special thanks to Leo Braudy, Rachel Brownstein, Paul Duguid, Bob Newsom, Barbara Nunberg, Scott Parker, and Tom Wasow, people I came back to over and over again for help in clarifying an idea.

I owe a debt as well to Phyllis Myers, the *Fresh Air* producer I've worked with for many years, and to Terry Gross and Danny Miller, who created and sustained the remarkable program that has been the setting for many of these pieces. (Not many language commentators get a better opening act than that one.) Peter Edidin, my editor at the *New York Times* Week in Review, has not only helped me to shape the pieces that appeared in the section, but has patiently instructed me in the stylistic intricacies of *Times*-speak. (In the end, though, I decided to edit the versions of the pieces contained here to eliminate the peculiarities of address that the *Times* requires—it seemed odd to be referring to the president as "Mr. Bush" on one page and simply as "Bush" on another.) Thanks, too, to my agent, Joe Spieler, and to Clive Priddle, my editor at PublicAffairs.

Finally, thanks as usual to Sophie Nunberg, who has inspired many of my pieces in her progress from toddlerhood to adolescence, as she and the English language come gradually and sometimes uneasily to terms. And to Michelle Carter I owe loving gratitude not just for her personal support and encouragement, but for reading over many of these pieces and offering me the benefit of her writerly good sense. Whatever the deficiencies of this book, it would have been a lot more pretentious and obscure if I hadn't had her judgment to draw upon.

[Going Nucular]

[Culture at Large]

Plastics!

We're all attuned to the word games that other people try to play on us—what we have to watch out for are the ones we play on ourselves. Consider the curious transformation of *plastic*. For the first part of the twentieth century, that word connoted all the blessings that science was bestowing on modern life. Then, forty years ago, it suddenly became the P-word, and synthetic materials started having to deny their paternity.

The American enchantment with synthetics began in the 1920s, when Bakelite caught on as a material for everything from fountain pens to telephones, and haute couture designers like Elsa Schiaparelli redeemed viscose from its chintzy associations under the new name of rayon. The name was taken from the French word for "beam of light" and set the pattern for later names like nylon, Dacron, Orlon, and Ban-lon.

Those were the glamour years of plastics. The transparent version of viscose called cellophane was such a success in both packaging and fashion that Cole Porter listed it among the superlatives of *You're the Top*, alongside the Coliseum, the Louvre Museum, Mickey Mouse, and a summer night in Spain. And in a 1940 poll to determine the most beautiful word in the English language, *cellophane* came in third, right behind *mother* and *memory*. Hardly a year went by that some new miracle fiber didn't capture the public imagination. Nylon took the world by storm when it made its debut at the World's Fair of 1939, where the DuPont pavilion featured a shapely Miss Chemistry reclining on a podium in nylon stockings.

Over the following decades, the press was full of exotic new names like Lucite, vinyl, Formica, Styrofoam, Dacron, and Saran Wrap, each of them replacing another natural material. By 1950, *Popular Mechanics* could show an illustration of a woman spraying a sleek couch with a garden hose, with the water running off into a drain in the floor, with the caption, "Because all her furniture is waterproof, the housewife of 2000 can do her daily cleaning with a hose."

But technological predictions have a way of going awry. Back in 1950, no one could have foreseen that little more than a decade later, *plastic* would become a problematic word. (And so, a little later on, would *housewife*.) The break in the filament was signaled in two events in 1963. In the fall of that year, DuPont introduced the leather substitute Corfam at the Chicago Shoe Show and went on to make the material the centerpiece of its 1964 World's Fair pavilion, a triumph of synthesis from its Tedlar roof and Delrin doorknobs to its Mylar curtains and Fabrilite seat upholstery.

DuPont had reason to be confident. Corfam was light and durable and could be cleaned with a wet sponge—it seemed a natural, if you'll excuse the expression. But Corfam was a marketing catastrophe. A few years later DuPont took a $100 million write-off and sold off its Corfam operation to a company in the People's Republic of Poland, where the fabric quickly became the cynosure of captive-nation haute couture.

People had good practical reasons for rejecting Corfam, which didn't breathe or break in the way leather did. But the material was also the victim of a more equivocal attitude toward synthetic products. As it happens, in fact, 1963 also recorded the first use of the word *plastic* to refer to something superficial or insincere. By 1967, the nation was snickering at the line in Mike Nichols's *The Graduate*, in which a skeptical young Dustin Hoffman received career advice from a family friend: "I just want to say one word to you.... Plastics!"

That line marked the end of America's innocent faith in the synthetic future: From then on, *plastic* would be charged with a curious ambiguity. For the hippies and later the greens, the word stood in for all the wastefulness and superficiality of American consumer culture. As Stephen Fenichell put it in his lively social history *Plastic: The Making of a Synthetic Century*, plastic embodies the features that people like to denigrate about the twentieth century—artificiality, disposability, and synthesis.

Frank Zappa sounded that note in his 1967 *Plastic People*: "I'm sure that love will never be / A product of plasticity." That was the progenitor of a line of musical plastiphobia that was carried on in songs like Radiohead's *Fake Plastic Trees* and Alanis Morissette's *Plastic*. ("You got a plastic girl in a plastic bed.... Got a plastic smile on a plastic face / But it's underneath that you can't erase.")

But the 1960s also saw the birth of a new kind of plastiphilia, which had less to do with the corporate triumphalism of DuPont's "Better Living Through Chemistry" than with the ironic detachment of pop art and the mods of Swinging London. That sensibility was what led performers to take names like Plastic Bertrand and the Plastic Ono Band. And it had its own anthems, from the Jefferson Airplane's *Plastic Fantastic Lover* to Björk's *Dear Plastic*, a paean to artifice: "Dear Plastic/Be proud/Don't imitate anything/ You're pure, pure, pure."

In the end, both parties prevailed. The plastiphiles left us with a new distinction between hip plastic and unhip plastic. Unhip plastic was AstroTurf, Lucite chandeliers, disposable diapers, and the double-knit polyester leisure suits that were leaving pills on the upholstery of discotheques across America. Hip plastic was girls in vinyl Mary Quant miniskirts dancing the Watusi (a song by the Orlons). It was the plastic chain-mail dresses of Paco Rabanne and the spandex outfits of David Bowie and the glam-rockers he spawned.

Unhip plastic was foam cups and cigarette wrappers that people dropped on the beach; hip plastic was the million square feet of polypropylene sheeting that Christo used to wrap a mile-long section of the Australian coast near Sydney. Needless to say, those distinctions have nothing to do with chemistry or environmental apprehensions—the same molecules can be unhip in car upholstery and hip in a Gucci bag.

But the plastiphobes had an effect, as well. Once *plastic* became a term of derision, people started to avoid the word to refer to the new materials that were coming out of labs. From the sixties on, *plastic* no longer meant any manufactured polymer, the way it had in the 1950s—now it only connotes glossy materials like vinyl, polystyrene, and Lucite. Ask people what their computer housings are made of, and they'll fumble for a name.

For that matter, the word *polyester* has been dropped from the advertising lexicon. People may still drape their bodies in it, but now it's sold as microfiber, or under brand names like Gore-Tex, Polar Fleece, and Eco-Spun—names free of any of the tacky, down-market evocations of *Saturday Night Fever*. And forty years after Corfam tanked, synthetic leather was back as pleather, the fabric of choice for animal-friendly performers like Britney Spears and Janet Jackson—with the P-word reduced to an unobtrusive prefix *p*. It's an efficient way of accommodating our aesthetic or ecological scruples about plastic—we merely call it something else and go on as before. It's just one word.

Keeping Ahead of the Joneses

You can tell a lot about an age from the way it adapts prefixes to its purposes. Take our enthusiasm for using *post-* in new ways. Sometimes it means "late" rather than "after," as in *postcapitalism*, and sometimes, as in *postmodernism*, it means something like "once more without feeling."

As it happens, the same sort of process has been going on more quietly with *pre-* at the other end of the scale. Time was, *pre-* chiefly meant "before," as in *prewar* or *prepubescent*. In recent years, though, the meaning of the prefix seems to be shifting to "in advance."

The world offers us preowned cars, preassembled furniture, precooked meals, prewashed denim, and preapproved loans. Hotels urge us to prebook our rooms (invariably more productive than postbooking them). At the airport gate, they announce preboarding and the VIPs and first-class passengers are already getting on the plane. It's an ideal prefix for an age that's preoccupied with getting a leg up on things.

The importance of getting an early advantage was behind the shift in the meaning of *preschool* about fifty or sixty years ago. Before that, the word could refer only to children too young to attend school. Then progressive educators drafted it into service as a new name for the nursery school, a name that brought to mind a place where toddlers frittered away their days in idle play. *Preschool* implied a more goal-directed curriculum—a "developmentally oriented readiness" program, as the 92nd Street Y in Manhattan puts it.

That's unquestionably a worthy object—it's implicit in the name Head Start, after all. But in the case of institutions like the 92nd Street Y, *preschool* is understood a bit more specifically than it normally is—it's really a shorthand for pre-pre-Harvard-Yale-or-Princeton. So it isn't surprising that parents go to considerable lengths to secure a place for their children on the first rung of that ladder.

"There are no bounds for what you do for your children," the Citigroup analyst Jack B. Grubman said in the e-mail message that suggested he might have traded a bullish rating on AT&T for help from his boss, Sanford Weill, in getting his two-year-old twins into the Y program. If that's correct, then few parents have a better right to make that claim.

In the earlier age of unapologetic privilege, a man making $20 million a year wouldn't have had to bother with such things— members of the coupon-clipping classes simply put their sons down at birth for Groton or Eton. Now, anxious parents with no strings to pull are obliged to enlist friends and family in a frenzy of dialing on the morning after Labor Day, as they desperately try to secure one of the limited places on the schools' applicant lists. "It's the most democratic way," explained Alix Friedman, the Y's director of public relations. Indeed, it seems to have become a tenet of modern egalitarianism that the fairest way to apportion scarce resources, whether nursery-school places or postseason tickets, is according to people's deftness in handling the speed-dial button. Life is getting to feel a lot like *Jeopardy*.

So it's natural that people should get indignant when some-one's caught cutting to the head of the line—not that most of us wouldn't have done the same if a pair of World Series tickets were in the balance.

That's what predestination comes down to in these postmeri-tocratic times; it's a matter of going through the motions of equal access at the same time you're frantically trying to game the system. Among all the denials and disclaimers that were mak-ing the rounds after Mr. Grubman's concession, in fact, the "but-ter-wouldn't-melt" award would have to go to Ms. Friedman's assertion that a million-dollar donation from Citigroup hadn't helped to grease the way for Grubman's twins. "No child is guar-anteed admission here," she said. "Every child—every child—goes through the same rigorous admissions process."

What the skeptics found hard to swallow about that wasn't just the implausibility of supposing that the Y accepted Citi-group's money and then said, "We'll get back to you on the Grubman kids"—or, what seems like an even bigger stretch, that a shrewd postcapitalist like Weill would have handed the Y a mil-lion bucks on pure spec. It's the claim that the Y evaluates its two-and-a-half-year-old applicants according to a rigorous ad-missions process, as if all those little Warburgs, Schiffs, Allens, and Stings had been chosen on merit alone. It reminds you that *precocious* is just the Latin for "precooked"—you wonder if there are objective tests that can preselect the toddlers who will rise like soufflés under the preschool's warm attentions.

Wouldn't the parents of a 92nd Street Y rejectee be happier if the Y just came out and said that the fix was in? Otherwise, it's a bit like being told that the passengers who are preboarding in first class were selected because they looked as if they would make the best use of the champagne, not because they paid more for their tickets.

It may be, as Nicholas Lemann suggests in *The Big Test: The Secret History of the American Meritocracy*, that the meritocratic system began to unravel when it ceased to be aimed at picking the best people for public service and became largely a matter of deciding how to hand out the goodies. What is clear is that opportunity is increasingly a matter of getting an early jump on things—of pretesting, preselection, preapproval, preadmission, and, not to be coy about it, prepayment. Or, as a letter I received the other day informed me, "You may already be a winner."

Caucasian Talk Circles

The recall has been getting all the ink, but the item on tomorrow's California ballot that has the most important national implications is what backers call the "racial privacy initiative," which sharply restricts the state's ability to classify people according to race.

Opponents of the measure argue that it will hamper efforts to gather information on discrimination, student progress, hate crimes, and health questions. Supporters defend it with the new rhetoric of color-blindness—they ridicule the stew of ethnic and racial identifications that students are required to tick off on University of California admission forms. As they put it, it's time to "junk a 17th-century racial classification system that has no place in 21st-century America."

They're not going to get much argument on that. But the classification system they want to sweep away is more of a modern creation than an antique one. And if the language of racial classification seems inconsistent and jumbled, that's the fault of the uneven social landscape we're asking it to map.

Those inconsistencies came to the surface in a recent story about a fifteen-year-old high-school freshman in Oakley, Califor-

Fresh Air commentary, October 6, 2003

nia, who had gathered 250 signatures to start a Caucasian club. If African Americans, Latinos, and Asians could have clubs to "teach them their cultures," as she put it, then why shouldn't whites have one as well?

That logic was plausible to a lot of people, including 87 percent of the respondents to a poll conducted by a Los Angeles TV station. And while others thought the club was an ill-conceived idea, a lot of them blamed the multiculturalists for setting a bad example. As *National Review*'s Jay Nordlinger put it, "A Caucasian club—ugh! Enough of the Balkanization of America. . . . It is the Left's fault. It is the fault of all of those who have insisted on the prominence—virtually the primacy—of race."

Actually, the most revealing word there is "ugh." What is it about the history of that quaint word *Caucasian* that makes even conservatives a little squeamish about seeing it in an organization's bylaws? As it happens, the word is exactly as old as the American nation. It was invented in 1776 by the German anthropologist Johannes Blumenbach, a disciple of Linnaeus, as the name of one of the four basic racial stocks of mankind—he chose *Caucasian* in the belief that the white race began its peregrinations when Noah's ark landed on Mount Ararat in the Caucasus.

By all rights, the Caucasian label should have vanished a long time ago, along with Mongoloid, Negroid, and the other categories of discredited racial theories. But it proved to be a conveniently genteel term for excluding people of the wrong sort. In fact Americans have rarely used *Caucasian* in its original anthropological meaning, which included not just Europeans but the peoples of the Middle East and North Africa. In 1919, the secretary of an immigration reform group remarked that the United States gave citizenship to many who were not Caucasians, including "Tartars, Finns, Hungarians, Jews, Turks, Syrians, Persians, Hindus, Mexicans, Zulus, Hottentots [and] Kafirs." The Finns and Hungarians were presumably ruled out because they didn't speak an Indo-European language; the Persians and Hindus because of low surface albedo.

By the 1920s, the word had become common in the "Caucasian clauses" of organizational bylaws and the restrictive housing covenants that became common in the North in the years following World War I. As late as 1947, a civil-rights report of the American Missionary Association said there was no immediate prospect of "a mass migration of Negroes, Jews, and other minorities into exclusively Caucasian areas." And when Jews were reclassified as Caucasians soon after that, it had more to do with a reevaluation of their effects on property values than with any new findings in physical anthropology.

Even now, that dispensation hasn't been extended to the other Semitic peoples. "It's not Arabs against Caucasians," explained CNN's anchor Jack Cafferty shortly after the September 11, 2001, attacks. It's unlikely he would have been tempted to put that as "Arabs against whites." When it comes to the crunch, *Caucasian* doesn't mean much more than "white people who play golf."

In fact the Caucasian label has become even more common in recent years, to the point where it's part of the active vocabulary of a high-school freshman. That's partly a response to the need for a term to pair with *African American*, another odd entry in the American racial lexicon. When *African American* was popularized in the late 1980s, it was supposed to suggest an identity defined by color rather than one defined by ancestry. But we don't use *African American* the way we use labels like *Italian American*, where we feel free to drop the *American* when the context makes it clear. We talk about an Italian neighborhood, but not an African one. The "African" of *African American* isn't a geographical label, it's just a prefix that means "black."

If we were being consistent, we'd contrast *African American* with *European American*. But that term has never caught on widely, probably because Europe is a more diverse place than Africa in the mental geography of most Americans. About the only people you see using *European American* are scholars and the modern racialists who have tricked out their programs in the language of multiculturalism. (A couple of years ago, an outfit called the European American Issues Forum persuaded the California legislature to proclaim a European American Heritage Month. That occasioned a lot less comment than if they'd called it White Heritage Month.)

Instead of *European American*, people use *Caucasian*, which seems to invest European descent with an objective scientific standing. That's specious, of course—if *African American* is a racial category masquerading as a cultural one, *Caucasian* is a cultural category in racial drag. But it can be a useful word to have around when you want to make a racial contrast without risking a charge of vulgar bias. When it was argued that the ballots used in some California counties discriminated against minority voters, Robert Novak asked on CNN, "Does that mean that the minority groups are not as able to use these ballots as the Caucasians?" The remark would have sounded a lot more confrontational if he had put it in terms of "whites."

The scientific-sounding cachet of *Caucasian* made the word the natural choice for the name of a high school club. To white adolescents in the California suburbs, the old ethnic identifications are remote and attenuated; that California high school student who wanted to start a Caucasian club described her own ancestry as American Indian, Hispanic, Dutch, German, Italian, and Irish—by that point, you're only talking about vague family lore. And mere whiteness is apt to strike the adolescents as boring—as the student put it on CNN, "Well, you ask the kids, what are you? They'll say white, but white, that's not a race."

To be sure, that explanation gets it backwards—if any of these is a racial category, it's white, not Caucasian. But confusion is endemic in the American language of race. We're always struggling to find racial labels that answer the question "what are you" with even-handed essences, but the labels keep catching their sleeves on disparities in the way we think about race itself. Racial classifications are like irregular verbs—they may be inconsistent, but they run too deep to be eliminated by decree.

Near Myths

I was struck by the difference in the words that the Bushes *père* and *fils* used in their tributes to Ted Williams. The elder Bush called Williams "a great hero," whereas his son used the phrase "a baseball legend." Of course it's understandable that the two would think of Williams differently. Williams was a personal hero to Bush senior, himself a talented ballplayer in New England and a wartime Navy pilot. But you wouldn't expect Williams's name to have had the same resonance for Bush II, who was a Texas schoolboy when Williams was finishing his career, and whose relationship to both baseball and combat has been exclusively managerial.

But there's a generational difference between those words, too. In the press tributes to Williams, *legend* outnumbered *hero* by better than five to one—and when the press did call Williams a hero, the stories generally added something about his service as a Marine pilot, as if his baseball achievements alone didn't entirely justify the label. Of course, some of that reflects a post–September 11 self-consciousness about using the word *hero*. But *legend* was nudging *hero* aside well before then. If you look at the way the press described players like Babe Ruth and Lou Gehrig between 1980 and 2000, you find that the use of *hero* declined by 50 percent, while the use of *legend* doubled.

That isn't to say that we've entirely left off expecting sports stars to be heroic—at least we seem to hold Barry Bonds accountable for imperfections of character that we're willing to overlook in Sean Penn or Mick Jagger. But modern fans are much too hip and too knowing to put up with the hero-worshipping panegyric of pre-World War II sportswriters like Grantland Rice. People are more comfortable with the flip, self-referential banter of the talk shows on ESPN and Fox Sports Network, where the operant slogan seems to be "We are not impressed."

There's a sign of that shift in the disappearance of those heroic titles that the press used to bestow on players. I'm not thinking of simple nicknames like Dizzy, Babe, or Yogi—there are still plenty of those around. But the modern media don't go in much for Homeric epithets like the Sultan of Swat, the Splendid Splinter, or the Yankee Clipper—and when they do, the titles usually have a postmodern edge to them. It's hard to imagine Grantland Rice immortalizing any of the 1927 Yankees with a label like the Big Unit.

For that matter, Grantland Rice would never have described any player as a legend, either, if only because back when he was writing, the word could only refer to a story from popular folklore, not the person who inspired it. The new meaning of the word originated with the phrase "a legend in one's own time," which was first used by Lytton Strachey to describe Florence Nightingale. But it wasn't until the 1970s or so that people began to use *legend* all by itself to refer to someone whose celebrity was especially long-lived.

That shift from *hero* to *legend* is the media's backhand way of celebrating their own power—the measure of someone's greatness now is not so much what he did as how long people kept talking about him. There can be unsung heroes, after all, but there are no unsung legends. And in fact the modern use of *legend* stands the traditional meaning of the word on its head. We never use the word to refer to someone whose fame is rooted in a genuine oral tradition—we don't talk about "aeronautical legend Icarus" or "transportation legend Casey Jones." On the contrary, the people we describe as legends now are the furthest thing from legendary in the literal sense of the word—they're people who have been the focus of media attention throughout their careers, the way Williams was. It's the media's way of investing their own creations with folkloric status.

It's true that there is a genuinely legendary aspect to Ted Williams's fame. At least it's certain that people would still be talking about him even if there had been no newspapers, radio, or TV around to document his accomplishments—if he'd played in the early era of the game, or if he'd been born with the wrong skin color to play major-league ball, like the literally legendary greats of the Negro Leagues. But *legend* has a leveling effect—it makes no distinction between people whose deeds are inherently memorable and celebrities who are pure media creations. Nose around in the press and you'll run into references to television legend Ed McMahon, entertainment legend Charo, modeling legend Twiggy, and pop legend Leo Sayer. It seems unfair to use the same label for Ted Williams and Leo Sayer—after all, the one had 2,654 career hits, and the other only had about two.

That semantic deflation is inevitable when we make celebrity the measure of achievement, particularly when celebrity is a commodity that's so easy to coin. In an age when everybody is famous for fifteen minutes, a legend is someone who has been in the limelight for half an hour. When the Yankees finished a spring training facility in Tampa, Florida, a couple of years ago the team christened it Legends Field. If the Yankees were renaming it now I expect they'd call it Icon Field or Avatar Alley. In fact they have my permission to rename it Heroes Field, just as soon as someone on the roster hits for a .400 season.

Lamenting Some Enforced Chastity

These are hard times for chastity. As Pope John Paul II pointed out in his remarks recently: "The life of chastity ... confutes the conventional wisdom of the world." And Eugene Clark, the rector of Saint Patrick's Cathedral in New York City, pointed to the difficulties that priests had in maintaining their vows in a "sex-saturated" society, where Americans are bombarded by images of "liberated sex all day long."

But chastity was problematic for both the Church and society at large well before Hugh Hefner and Larry Flynt filed their first business plans. You can see that in the declining use of the words *chaste* and *chastity* themselves. In modern times those words tend to be used chiefly in a metaphorical way—you see a lot more references to chaste architecture or a chaste prose style than to chaste men and women.

The fact is that we moderns are uncomfortable about using words that associate sexual continence with spiritual purity. We've lost sight of the connection that used to be implicit in words like *chasten* and *chastise*, which originally had the sense of "make chaste," or "purify." (For that matter, the word *castrate* comes from the same Latin root—it's just a more draconian way of getting at the same end.)

Fresh Air Commentary, May 2, 2002

Not surprisingly, the eclipse of *chastity* has blurred the original meaning of the word. It's true that chastity has always
involved abstaining from illicit sex. But chastity wasn't the same
thing as virginity: You could become chaste even if you had
already had sexual experience. As Saint Augustine put it in a
famous prayer, "Lord, give me chastity and continence, but not
now." For that matter, chastity didn't necessarily rule out sex
within marriage, so long as it was free of prurience or concupis-
cence. "Moor, she was chaste"—that's how Aemilia tells Othello
that his wife, Desdemona, was innocent of the infidelities that he
had imagined.

By the eighteenth century, though, chastity was regarded as a
minor virtue, and one associated chiefly with women, as the secular double standard came into its own. Samuel Johnson wrote of
one vain, insipid country wife that she had no virtue but chastity.
And over the last hundred years, people have pretty much bailed
out on using the word *chaste* to describe sexual continence—
instead they've appropriated the word *celibate*, which originally
meant only unmarried.

But some people have been trying to revive the word *chastity*.
On the Web, it comes up a lot in the sites for organizations promoting sexual abstinence, a movement that's on a roll right now.
Recently, for example, a House committee authorized an addi-
tional $50 million for "abstinence only" sex-education, this in addi-
tion to the half-billion dollars in state and federal funds that the
programs have already received. The programs encourage teens
to swear off sex until marriage and provide no information about
birth control, abortion, or gay and lesbian sex, on the grounds
that such information might put ideas into adolescents' heads.
The sites of the abstinence-only groups warn adolescents about

the dangers of condoms and offer them suggestions as to how to restrain their sexual urges—one provides helpful links to the Amazon.com pages where they can order Scrabble and Trivial Pursuit.

But trying to resuscitate an unfashionable word is like trying to revive an old folk dance or costume—people invariably get the details wrong. The abstinence-only movement tends to talk about chastity as if it were merely the equivalent of virginity. The movement asks adolescents to sign vows pledging to remain "chaste until marriage"—there's no sense that chastity might be a state that you could maintain even after you've entered a committed sexual relationship, the way Desdemona did. And they often talk about the loss of chastity as an irrevocable step. As one group puts it: "Chastity is a lifestyle. One date may be too late." Saint Augustine would have cut teens more slack than that.

As it happens, though, the abstinence-only organizations aren't the only ones who are contributing to the comeback of the word *chastity*. There's an odd mirror of their preoccupations in the Web sites put up by people who are into chastity as a source of sexual stimulation, by means of devices that prevent any kind of sexual activity until the wearer is released by the keyholder. For women, the sites offer new variations on the chastity belt (which by the way was actually invented during the Italian Renaissance, not the Crusades, and which was probably very rarely used until its rediscovery by modern fetishists). For men there are a variety of cuffs, sheaths, and cages that achieve an analogous effect by what appear to be calculatedly uncomfortable means. Curiously, enthusiasts use the word *chastisement* to describe the process of putting your associate into one of these contrivances. It isn't the normal use of the word, but it does have etymology on its side.

Given their druthers, I expect most people would prefer to curb their sexual urges with a brisk game of Scrabble. Still, the chastisement sites do capture something of the old sense of chastity as an austere spiritual practice. And unlike the abstinence-only movement, they share something else of the Roman Catholic Church's view of chastity: They don't pretend everyone has the vocation for it.

Stolen Words

The striking thing about plagiarism is how rarely anybody has anything original to say about it. Including that, let me hasten to add. Or at least that's pretty much how it seems as you look back over the history of literary scandals—the indignant accusations, the protestations of innocent error, and above all the puzzling gratuitousness of the crime. I'm not talking about a student who goes on the Internet to buy a term paper for a course he hasn't attended all semester. That may be reprehensible, but it isn't mysterious. But why do competent and successful writers stoop to copying unattributed passages from other published works— often works that are well enough known so that detection is pretty likely? And why are the passages they steal so often banal and unnecessary?

The answer's different for different writers. Why did Samuel Taylor Coleridge appropriate numerous passages of German philosophy in his *Biographia Literaria*, most of them digressions that add very little to the work? Biographers have suggested that Coleridge did it because he was blocked, or depressed, or had a self-destructive impulse. But you could hardly claim that Stephen Ambrose suffered from writer's block, and there's no evidence that he's self-destructive. In part his plagiarism seemed to be simply a sign of arrogance, a sense that his vast popular audience would neither know nor care if he stole the words of some lesser-known academic historian.

But in Ambrose's case, the deficiency was as much aesthetic as moral. Take these sentences from Ambrose's best-seller *The Wild Blue*, one of many that came almost verbatim from a book by the historian Thomas Childers: "Up, up, up he went, until he got above the clouds...B–24's, glittering like mica, were popping up out of the clouds ... ." You wonder why an author would want to pass that bit off as his own—not just purple writing, but somebody else's shade of purple. It's the sign of a writer who's deaf to his own voice—and in fact, of a writer who doesn't really care whether he has a voice at all.

In Doris Kearns Goodwin's case, though, the plagiarisms are more puzzling, not just because she's a better writer than Ambrose, but because the passages she stole are so pedestrian. Here's one of a number of sentences from Goodwin's 1987 book *The Fitzgeralds and the Kennedys* that were lifted more-or-less verbatim from Lynne McTaggart's 1983 biography of Kathleen Kennedy: "Hardly a day passed without a newspaper photograph of little Teddy taking a snapshot with his camera held upside down, or the five Kennedy children lined up on a train or bus."

Why would anybody bother to steal such an ordinary sentence? Goodwin's explanation was that the borrowing wasn't intentional—she said she had taken notes in longhand when she was preparing the book, then lost track of which bits she had written herself. That appeal to muddled note-taking is a familiar motif in these affairs. It's the same explanation Alex Haley gave in 1976 when it turned out that his book *Roots* included numerous passages from Harold Courlander's novel *The African*. And Coleridge's nephew Henry offered the same defense for his uncle's literary derelictions—he explained that Coleridge was a very sloppy note-taker, who mixed his own thoughts with "the thoughts of others, which he later failed to recognize as such."

But this sort of explanation is hard to credit, particularly in Goodwin's case. Suppose you were taking notes in longhand from a biography and you ran across a sentence like "Hardly a day passed without a newspaper photograph of little Teddy taking a snapshot with his camera held upside down, or the five Kennedy children lined up on a train or bus." You wouldn't write that down word-for-word; you'd put down something like "p. 25 Frequent pix of Ted w/ upside-down Brownie." And it strains credulity to imagine that Goodwin could have written down forty or fifty such sentences verbatim, then forgotten that they weren't her own.

But then, why did Goodwin do it? Actually, my own suspicion is that it may very well have been inadvertent, at least on her part—I'll bet that one of her research assistants copied some of the sentences from McTaggart's book in the course of summarizing it, and that Goodwin just dumped the assistant's summaries into her book without checking them against the source. And if she didn't 'fess up when the plagiarism was discovered, it might be because she didn't want to admit to not having read the sources herself, or what's worse, to having cribbed her prose from a research assistant.

Whatever the truth is, though, we can't let Goodwin off the hook. It may be that authors like Goodwin and Ambrose have become less like writers and more like managers coordinating the activity of their staffs. But as other recent events have reminded us, CEOs are still responsible for everything that goes on on their watch. The American Historical Association dropped the clause in its statement on plagiarism that said that there had to be an intent to deceive—as an official of the association explained, "It's plagiarism whether you intended to do so or not." And we haven't yet gotten to the point where we'll allow our historians to claim credit for the words of paid researchers or ghostwriters or speechwriters, the way we allow Jack Welch or George W. Bush to do. In the end, after all, that's all an author is, somebody whose words we pay to read.

Beating Their Brows

Highbrow and *lowbrow* were coined at the end of the nineteenth century as nods to the popular belief that physiognomy was a sure guide to intellectual capacity. The words themselves were lowbrow inventions, which novelists tended to put into the mouths of roughnecks or uneducated characters—Sinclair Lewis's Babbitt describes a dinner as "a real sure-enough highbrow affair."

But *middlebrow* had a more genteel parentage when it was coined a generation later, as the elite's way of disparaging the tastes of middle-class consumers of culture, in their earnest efforts at self-betterment. As a 1925 article in *Punch* put it, middlebrows were "people who are hoping that someday they will get used to the stuff they ought to like."

Middlebrow had its cultural moment just after World War II. In 1949, *Harper's* editor Russell Lynes wrote an influential article called "Highbrow-Middlebrow-Lowbrow," and a few years later, Dwight Macdonald wrote a famous polemic called "Masscult and Midcult," a vituperative attack on middlebrow culture. That was all it took to set off a kind of national parlor game, as critics set about putting everything into its appropriate pigeonhole. Highbrow was Ezra Pound, the Berlin Philharmonic, and John Dewey; lowbrow was Mickey Spillane, Guy Lombardo, and Walter Winchell; middlebrow was Edna Ferber, Andre Kostelanetz, and Walter Lippmann.

The distinctions were crude and simplistic, the way they always are in these listing exercises that capture the public fancy every so often—U and non-U, camp and kitsch, modern and postmodern, wired and tired. But there were serious issues at stake. For Macdonald, middlebrow was the safe, smug enemy of great art—in his words, it was "the tide line where the decisive struggles for survival take place between higher and lower organisms." That view appealed to many intellectuals on both the right and the left. They made common cause against the tide of middlebrow art, in America's last great eructation of cultural snobbery.

Those were the echoes that Jonathan Franzen evoked when he demurred from appearing on *Oprah* for fear he might compromise his status as a writer in what he called "the high-art literary tradition." Franzen later apologized, but the word "high" still stuck in some people's craw. "High," "middle," "low"—those old hierarchies sound out of date these days. We may still be interested in distinctions of taste and quality, but we aren't comfortable about arranging them vertically anymore. The British art critic Robert Hewison once said that when he was growing up, culture was organized like a pyramid, but that somewhere along the way it got tipped over on its side.

One reason for this is that patterns of cultural consumption aren't as closely linked to class as they used to be. Back in 1953, the critic Clement Greenberg could write, "Middlebrow . . . is born . . . out of the desire of newly ascendant social classes to rise culturally." That might have been true in an age when people were proudly lining their shelves with the latest selections of the Britannica great books or the Literary Guild. But the people who tune in to Oprah's book club seem to be more interested in personal growth than social advancement. Nowadays, after all, literary discernment doesn't give you much of a leg up socially. There's a passage in Martin Amis's novel *The Information* where one of the characters observes how literary taste degrades as you walk up the aisle of an airplane. In economy people are reading *Middlemarch*, in business they're reading John Grisham, and in first they're just sleeping and eating caviar.

Then too, nowadays we all do our cultural shopping from the same outlets. The *New Yorker* writer John Seabrook argued in a recent book that the old distinctions of high, middle, and low have been superseded by a new amalgam that he calls Nobrow. Nobrow is the creation of the high-powered cultural marketing that gives us blockbuster museum shows, music megastores, and crossover bestsellers. You can hear that in the disappearance of that condescending phrase "mass culture" that mid-twentieth-century critics used to rail about—now it's all "popular culture," which suggests an event with festival seating.

The new cultural scene doesn't lend itself very well to those old categories of brow. You could still appeal to the highbrow-middlebrow distinction if you're talking about the difference between Eliot Carter and the Three Tenors. But how do you sort out the highbrows and the middlebrows in the world of pop, which is where American musical culture is really enacted now? Beck versus Billy Joel? Björk versus Sarah Brightman? What's left of the notion of highbrow art, when there's a Norman Rockwell show on exhibit right now at the Guggenheim? And however Franzen may think of himself, he isn't really in a highbrow liter-

ary tradition, no more than novelists like Dave Eggars or Michael
Chabon. If you want undiluted highbrow nowadays, you have to
send abroad for it. W. G. Sebald, Milan Kundera, Umberto Eco—
those are the writers who can still make you feel you should have
paid more attention in eleventh grade.

You still hear the word *middlebrow* from time to time, but it
sounds increasingly irrelevant and desperate. There was an article
in the *Wall Street Journal* not long ago dismissing Christiane
Amanpour as a middlebrow, which begged the question of what
a highbrow war correspondent would sound like—would allusions to Thucydides help?

In fact those mid-century attacks on the middlebrow sound
embarrassing now. The fulminations about the tradition of high
art, the horror of middle-class vulgarity, the fixation on distin-
guishing between the great and the merely near-great—in retrospect, it all smacks of the same humorless piety and cultural
insecurity that critics were assailing in the self-improving middle
classes. When you come down to it, middlebrow was always a
pretty middlebrow idea.

Prurient Interests

A couple of years ago I had a call from a lawyer working with a local public defender's office. His client had been arrested when he was stopped on the street late at night with a length of chain attached to a padlock in his pocket. The arrest was pursuant to an old section of the penal code that makes it a felony to carry any of a long list of weapons including a "slungshot," an archaic term that one 1951 dictionary defined as "a weapon used chiefly by criminals consisting of a weight attached to a flexible handle or strap."

The attorney wanted my help in filing a motion arguing that the statute clashes with a basic principle of interpretation: The law ought to be written in words that give what lawyers call "fair and reasonable notice of the conduct prohibited." That seemed fair enough to me; when you're telling people what they can and can't do, you ought to use language they can be expected to understand. Of course you could say that the wording of the penal code hardly matters in a case like this: People don't ordinarily consult a statute book before they go out at night with a chain and lock in their pocket. But by that line of argument we may as well go back to writing statutes in Latin. (I know several people in the classics department who would welcome the work.)

Fresh Air Commentary, May 28, 2002

Obscure legal language can sometimes have a much broader effect than in that *slungshot* case. Take the word *prurient*. In a famous 1973 decision, the Supreme Court held that the standard for judging obscenity is "whether, to the average person, applying contemporary community standards, the dominant theme of the material . . . appeals to prurient interest." With minor variations, that formula has been widely used ever since then. It's an odd way to put things—asking the average person to judge whether something "appeals to prurient interest" when the average person probably doesn't know the word *prurient* in the first place. I have an image of Larry Flynt stopping passersby to ask their opinion of the latest number of *Hustler*: "What do you think? Not too prurient, is it?"

It's true that *prurient* is far from being an obsolete word like *slungshot*. But even people who know the word often seem to have no clear idea of its meaning. *Prurient* is originally from the Latin root for "itch," and modern dictionaries define it in terms of an "unusual" or "unhealthy" interest in sex. So people have prurient minds when they have an unhealthy interest in sex, and things are prurient when they arouse that sort of interest. But you find a lot of people using *prurient* just as a vague synonym for "lewd" or "erotic." At the 2 Live Crew obscenity trial in St. Petersburg, Florida, in 1990, the prosecutor charged that the rap group had "incited the crowd to prurient behavior." And some years ago, Massachusetts Governor Edward King claimed that a new pornography law would protect children from "perverted persons who would coerce them into committing prurient acts."

Those people are plainly Unclear on the Concept. Acts and behavior can't be prurient in and of themselves, not if you use the word correctly. But then it's unlikely that any of these people ever looked the word up—they just guessed at its meaning on the basis of having seen it in one context, that Supreme Court definition of obscenity. In fact, that single clause of the Court's definition accounts for more than half the occurrences of the word in the press. If not for that decision, *prurient* would probably be as rare a word as *concupiscent* or *nugatory*.

The problem with building law around obscure words like *prurient* isn't just that it fails to give fair and reasonable notice. The fact is that it's hard for *anybody* to say exactly what a word like *prurient* means today, not excluding lexicographers. Lawyers tend to think that learned words like *prurient* are somehow more precise than everyday items like *lustful* or *dirty*. Actually it's the opposite. That fuzziness about the meaning of *prurient* is typical of words that live in the margins of the language—people don't encounter them often enough to get a clear idea of what they mean. The more closely an expression is associated with a unique situation, like the Supreme Court's obscenity definition, the harder it is to pry out its general meaning. Take *caisson*, *madding*, and *petard*. Everybody's heard them in a single famous setting, but how many people can tell you with confidence what all of them mean?

"I know it when I see it." That's how Justice Potter Stewart responded in 1964 when he was asked to define obscenity. And in fact that's pretty much what the Court wound up saying when it slipped that obscure word *prurient* into its decision—it left prosecutors free to define obscenity however they liked. In the end, the Court's definition would have been more precise and consistent with the standards of real communities if it had defined obscenity by saying that it was a question of whether the work in question appealed to people with dirty minds. But then they wouldn't have sounded like judges.

[War Drums]

When Words Fail

Twice during the days following the terrorist attacks I listened on TV as witnesses to the World Trade Center calamity broke down, unable to continue their accounts. On both occasions the interviewers waited during a moment of awkward silence, then finished the sentences for the witnesses.

We feel conflicting urges at a moment like this. On the one hand, we hold that there are times when words ought to fail us, that there are things so horrible that silence is the only language for them. "Indescribable," "unutterable," "unspeakable"—those were the words that kept coming to mind as we struggled to comprehend what had happened.

But we share those reporters' discomfort with dead air, too. It may be that language can't do justice to the horror of experience, but it's the only game in town. So we all sat rapt as the networks kept running the same awful video clips under a babble of wan descriptions. "Shocking," "horrific," "terrible," "like a battlefield"—as if the repetition would eventually render the reality as familiar and banal as the language itself.

Language seemed to fail us, too, as a vehicle for expressing our sense of outrage. The popular press had it relatively easy—

the San Francisco *Examiner*'s front page the day after the attack showed a color picture of the World Trade Center explosion under the one-word screamer "Bastards!," which was something we all needed to get off our chests. But that approach wasn't an option for those to whom the public was looking for a more considered judgment. The official condemnations sounded oddly stilted. Both Gray Davis and Charles Schumer called the attacks "dastardly," a word that tends to bring to mind a mustachioed Gilbert and Sullivan villain, not a crazed zealot. It occurred to me that they might have seized on the word because of its sound associations, but in that case I preferred the *Examiner*'s version.

But other officials took the same anachronistic tone. President Bush called the attacks "despicable," which has a primly Victorian sound to it. A TV commentator described the acts as "nefarious," another Gilbert and Sullivan word. And numerous people used "infamy," which already sounded old-fashioned when President Franklin D. Roosevelt used it in describing the Pearl Harbor attack back in 1941.

You could hear that Victorian note, as well, in the condemnations of the hijackers as "craven" and as "faceless cowards," as if the most damning thing you could say about them is that they behaved dishonorably. Surprise attacks on unarmed civilians are repugnant by any moral standard. But "cowardly" doesn't explain that suicidal fanaticism—indeed you wish that some of the hijackers had chosen to chicken out when the time came to throw their lives away.

It was all strikingly different from the language we use to condemn other sorts of murderous outrages. The Unabomber was demented and the Columbine killings were senseless; nobody would have thought of describing either as infamous or dastardly.

True, everyday words might seem insufficient to describe an experience of this magnitude, at least for people and publications who are speaking for the historical record. Even "tragedy" felt too slight, vitiated by years of tabloid overexposure. But the contemporary language hasn't wholly lost its moral bearings. We still have resources that are up to rendering the enormity of the attacks, as well as words can ever hope to do: *ghastly, monstrous,* or *enormity* itself.

In the wake of the attacks, though, official America needed something else: language that would reassert control of a world that had gotten terrifyingly out of hand. Victorian indignation is ideal for that purpose—it evokes the moral certainties of a simpler age, when the line between civilization and barbarism was clearly drawn, and powerful nations brooked neither insult nor injury from lesser breeds without the law. This may be the first war of the twenty-first century, as President Bush has said. But its rhetoric has its roots in the nineteenth.

A Name Too Far

Recently, the White House was forced to apologize for the President's description of the campaign against terrorism as a "crusade," when it was pointed out that the word still evokes unpleasant historical memories among Muslim nations. Then the Administration blundered again when it dubbed the campaign Operation Infinite Justice, a name that seemed to some Muslims to promise what only Allah could deliver. The Pentagon quickly redesignated the buildup Operation Enduring Freedom, a name that manages to be both grandiose and dangerously ambiguous—you can be sure that some parties will see an interest in translating it so that *freedom* comes out as something that has to be endured.

That wasn't a problem that anyone had to worry about when the American military first started to give names to operations during World War II. Operations back then bore nondescript names like Avalanche, Market Garden, Mulberry, and of course Overlord, the name personally selected by Winston Churchill for the Normandy invasion. That name may have conveyed "a sense of majesty and patriarchal vengeance," as the historian David Kahn put it, but it was singularly uninformative about the mis-

San Jose *Mercury News*, September 30, 2001

sion. In fact Churchill himself urged that names be carefully chosen so as not to suggest the character of the operation, particularly after British intelligence intercepted references to a German operation called Sealion and guessed that it was a plan to invade Britain.

The Allied operation names were kept strictly secret, to the point where even an inadvertent mention could trigger an alarm. A few weeks before D-Day, the names Utah, Omaha, and Overlord showed up as answers in the London *Daily Telegraph's* crossword puzzle. Officers from MI5 rushed to Surrey to interview the schoolteacher who had composed the puzzle, but the whole business turned out to be a bizarre coincidence.

It wasn't until after the war that names like Overlord and Avalanche became household words, not to mention the model for the names of hundreds of movies, from *Operation Pacific* to *Operation Petticoat*. At that point the War Department realized there could be an advantage in creating a new category of unclassified operation nicknames for public-relations purposes. Even so, most of the postwar names were no more descriptive than the secret code names of World War II. President Eisenhower sent the Marines to Lebanon in 1957 under the name Operation Blue Bat, and the military operations in Vietnam tended to have names like End-Sweep, Pocket Money, and Abilene.

True, generals occasionally picked operation names that had more martial connotations, but that could backfire. When General Ridgeway named one Korea operation Killer, the State Department complained that he had soured the ongoing negotiations with the Chinese. Fifteen years later in Vietnam, General Westmoreland was forced to rename Operation Masher when President Johnson objected that the name didn't reflect the

administration's "pacification emphasis." And the press came
down on the Reagan administration when it dubbed the invasion
of Grenada Operation Urgent Fury, which seemed an excessively
bellicose title for a mission to rescue some medical students on a
Caribbean island with a police force smaller than the San Jose
Police Department.

The unhappy experience with the name Urgent Fury brought
home just how important an operation name could be in deter-
mining the public perception of a military action. By the late
1980s, the administration was choosing its operation names with
the media in mind. When the U.S. sent troops to Panama in 1989,
the Bush administration named the operation Just Cause. The
name irked some critics who had reservations about the legiti-
macy of the invasion—*The New York Times* ran an editorial on the
name entitled "Operation High Hokum." But a number of news
anchors picked up on the phrase "just cause" to describe the invasion, which encouraged the Bush and Clinton administrations to
make a policy of using tendentious names for their military
actions.

Operation Just Cause was followed by Operations Desert
Shield and Desert Storm, the first time the word "operation" was
swollen to apply to a full-blown war. Those were followed in
quick succession by Restore Hope in Somalia, Uphold Democracy
in Haiti, and operations in the Balkans that went by names like
Shining Hope, Determined Force, and Provide Promise. ("Provide" is a favorite element in these names—since 1989, we have
had operations called Provide Promise, Provide Refuge, Provide
Hope, Provide Transition, Provide Comfort, and Provide Relief.)

All of this has turned the naming of operations into a delicate
art. In an article a few years ago in the quarterly of the U.S. Army

War College, Lieutenant Colonel Gregory Sieminski offered several naming guidelines. First, he said, make the name meaningful. Don't waste a public relations opportunity—remember that the operation name is the first bullet in the war of images. Second, identify and target the critical audience—decide whether your name is intended to fire up the troops, win domestic support, allay the concerns of other nations, or intimidate the enemy. And finally, make it concise and memorable—find a name that vividly evokes the characteristics of the operation that you want people to focus on.

Those guidelines are good advice whether you're naming a military operation or a new SUV: It all comes down to branding. And it's no accident that the new-style names like Just Cause were introduced around the same time the cable news shows started to label their coverage of major stories with catchy names and logos. That practice began back in 1979 when ABC packaged its special coverage of the Iran hostage crisis as a late-night program called *America Held Hostage*, which later evolved into *Nightline*. But it was left to CNN and then the other cable news networks to routinely banner every major story, high or low. War in the Gulf, Death of a Princess, Flashpoint Kosovo, Boy in the Middle (that was Elián), Investigating the President, Power, Politics, and Pardons, The Search for Chandra Levy.

Like the Pentagon's operation names, the networks' titles suggest a master narrative for what might otherwise seem a disorderly stream of events. It's a convenient way of packaging stories like Elián Gonzáles or the Marc Rich pardon, which do have the feel of real-life miniseries. But the current crises are too far-reaching and open-ended to be comfortably wrapped by any banner.

You could see the networks struggling to find a unifying

theme for their coverage as they went from one banner to another: Assault on America, America Unites, America Rising, America on Alert, America Fights Back. But the pathos of the slogans seemed to diminish the enormity of the attacks and the events they had set in motion, from New York and Washington to Vero Beach, Florida, to Islamabad to Wall Street. And who knows where else, as events run their unpredictable course.

But at least the networks can keep reframing their narrative from one day to the next. The military has to come up in advance with a name for an "operation" that is going to be waged over many years in many different theaters, and whose outcome would be kindly described as murky. I think of the lines from Robinson Jeffers's *I Shall Laugh Purely*:

> *History falls like rocks in the dark,*
> *All will be worse confounded soon.*

"Operation Enduring Freedom" was not an auspicious choice. Even if you set aside its ambiguity, the name would have made Churchill uneasy. He was partial to naming operations after Roman gods, war heroes, or famous racehorses—words with a vaguely heroic rumble that didn't actually suggest anything about the goals of the mission. And he warned specifically against using words that imply an "overconfident sentiment." He knew as well as anyone how history delights in throwing unforeseen ironies our way.

Beleaguered Infidel

Listening to the video of Osama bin Laden that was released after the United States began its attack on Afghanistan, I was struck by the way the interpreter had him calling President Bush the "head of the infidels" and insisting that the "army of infidels" must leave the land of Mohammed. *Infidel* is such a quaint word in English that I wondered whether it was a fair translation.

With the help of an Egyptian colleague, I checked out the Arabic version of bin Laden's message. He had used the word *kaafir*, which does indeed translate as "infidel." *Kaafir* is one of those elastic terms that can stretch from out-and-out heathens to the heretics in the apartment upstairs. (The word exists in Hebrew, too, as *kofer*.) But in its strict meaning, *kaafir* refers to non-Muslims, particularly when they're considered confrontationally.

Muslim scholars divide the world between the *Dar-al-Kufr*, the land of the kaafirs, and the *Dar-al-Islam*, the land of the Muslims, with the *Dar-al-Harb*, or land of war, in the contested middle. In theory, *Dar-al-Islam* would be the Muslim counterpart to our word *Christendom*, but that word is pretty antiquated, too. The concept of Christendom hasn't played much of a role in the Western psyche since the Poles and Germans turned back the

Turkish armies at the siege of Vienna in 1683, the last time Muslim power was ever a serious threat to the West.

That seems to be the story with a lot of the words that translators use to render the language of Islamic fundamentalism—they have a musty medieval sound. When someone talks about infidels, I have an image of the characters in *Ivanhoe* who were always dashing off to the Holy Land to fight the Saracen infidel. In fact it was an old-fashioned word even by Shakespeare's time. He used it occasionally, particularly in the phrase "Turks and infidels," but he wouldn't have taken it seriously.

In Modern English, *infidel* isn't a word we ever use in earnest. People may style themselves infidels to suggest their defiance of some ruling orthodoxy. But it's a sign of how thoroughly our culture has been secularized that not even Jerry Falwell or Pat Robertson would use the word to describe nonbelievers, whatever their sexual orientation. It's like calling someone a pagan or heathen—it makes you sound like a sergeant-major out of a Kipling story. That was the weirdest thing about Falwell's rant about all the people who had brought the September 11 attacks down on America's head—he said it was the fault of "the pagans, the abortionists, the feminists, the gays and lesbians, . . . [and] the ACLU." True, there are some people around who like to style themselves pagans, but to most Americans, that word was a tip-off that Falwell wasn't simply being intolerant—he was living in some other century.

In fact the only time we still hear *infidel* used literally is when it's put into the mouths of swarthy villains. That's what was so odd about hearing the word in the voice-over translation of bin Laden's video. It sounded like something from an Indiana Jones movie: "Die, infidel dog!" *Infidel* may have started its life as a home-grown English word, but it's ending its days as a translation. Whether it's ominous or comic, it isn't a notion we use ourselves.

That's always the problem when you try to translate across a cultural divide—the words may be there, but they echo differently in the other person's room. The difficulty can cut both ways. A couple of weeks ago the White House had to apologize when President Bush offhandedly described the war on terrorism as a "crusade." Americans use that word without paying much attention to its origins, and we tend to forget that it has the root for "cross" buried in it, particularly when our Latin is shaky. But in Arabic, *crusade* translates as *al-hamalat as-salibiyya*, or "campaign of the cross," and it can still evoke some vivid historical memories. It was disconcerting to hear bin Laden throw the term back in an utterly literal way, referring to Bush as a "big crusader." For us, that's a word you can only apply to a courageous politician, a cartoon rabbit, or a World War II British tank.

It all underscores the problem that the U.S. faces as it tries to persuade the Muslim world that it isn't engaged in a religious war. Things are bound to be misunderstood—you think of what Islamic fundamentalists are likely to make of the people at ballparks singing *God Bless America* during the seventh-inning stretch, and how hard it would be to explain to them that it's really an Irving Berlin show tune. You wonder how there could be any accommodation or understanding between the two sides, when they hear the same words so differently.

In the end, though, it's hard to believe that communication is hopeless. Not long ago I was talking about Bush's "crusade" gaffe with a friend who teaches medieval Arabic history. Actually, she told me, if you wanted to do justice to "crusade" the way Bush used the word, you wouldn't translate it with the Arabic phrase that means "campaign of the cross." You'd use that word *jihad*. *Jihad* does have the meaning of a religious war, and in fact it was used to describe the military response to the crusades. But like *crusade*, it can also mean any kind of personal moral struggle. "These days," she said, "my jihad is being department vice-chair."

That made *jihad* feel a little less alien to me, and with it the corner of the Muslim mind that it inhabits. You wonder if the worlds are really so different that there can't be any translation between them. It reminded me of what a translator told me once. Verbatim translations tend to sound odd, particularly when they have to bridge a vast cultural gulf. But if you root around you'll usually find some other word that suggests a common point of understanding. If you're a translator, he said, you have to believe that when it comes to the crunch, people can always find something to talk about. And sometimes the translation that takes people at their literal word is the one that winds up being unfaithful.

It All Started with Robespierre

The *Washington Post* recently disclosed that the global head of news for Reuters had written an internal memo asking reporters to avoid describing the airplane hijackers as terrorists. As he explained, "One man's terrorist is another man's freedom fighter." And since then, Reuters dispatches have avoided using *terrorism* unless they were quoting someone.

Given the circumstances, Reuters's scruples seem misplaced— there are times when even-handedness can tip over into moral abdication. But the Reuters policy actually goes back more than twenty years, and reflects the equivocal history of the word itself.

Terrorism is one of those terms like *crusade*, which began its life at a particular historical moment, before losing its capital letter to become a common noun. In 1792, the Jacobins came to power in France and initiated what we call the Reign of Terror and what the French call simply *La Terreur*. The Jacobin leader, Robespierre called terror "an emanation of virtue" and added that "Terror is nothing but justice, prompt, severe and inflexible." And in the months that followed, the severe and inflexible justice of the guillotine severed 12,000 counterrevolutionary heads before it got around to abbreviating Robespierre himself.

San Francisco *Chronicle*, October 28, 2001

Of course, not everyone shared Robespierre's enthusiasm for the purifying effects of terror. One of the first writers to use *terrorist* in English was Edmund Burke, that implacable enemy of the French Revolution, who wrote in 1795 of "those hell-hounds called terrorists [who] are let loose on the people."

For the next 150 years, *terrorism* led a double life—a justifiable political strategy to some, an abomination to others. The Russian revolutionaries who assassinated Czar Alexander II in 1881 used the word proudly. And in 1905, Jack London described terrorism as a powerful weapon in the hands of labor, though he warned against harming innocent people.

But for the press and most of the public, *terrorist* connoted bomb-throwing madmen. Politicians weren't above using the word as a brush to tar socialists and radicals of all stripes, whatever their views of violence. When President William McKinley was assassinated by an anarchist in 1901, Congress promptly passed legislation that barred known anarchists from entering the United States.

By the mid-twentieth century, terrorism was becoming associated more with movements of national liberation than with radical groups, and the word was starting to acquire its universal stigma. One of the last groups willing to describe itself as terrorist was a Zionist organization called Lehi (*Lohamei Herut Israel*), known earlier as the Stern Gang, who killed dozens of people when they set off a bomb in the King David Hotel in Jerusalem in 1946.

Most of the Third-World movements that resorted to political violence in the 1950s and 1960s preferred terms like "freedom fighters" or "guerrillas" or "mujahedeen." *Terrorist* was reserved for use as a condemnation by the colonial powers. That's the point when news organizations started to become circumspect about using the word to describe groups like the Irish Republican Army, the Ulster Defense Association, or the African National Congress. Using the word seemed to be taking sides, and perhaps a little imprudent—particularly when you consider that former "terrorists" like Nelson Mandela and Menachem Begin ended their careers as winners of the Nobel Peace Prize.

By the 1980s, *terrorism* was being applied to all manner of political violence. There was a flap over the word in 1989 when the *New York Times* editor A. M. Rosenthal attacked Christopher Hitchens for refusing to describe the fatwah against Salman Rushdie as terrorism. Hitchens had a good point. The fatwah may have been repugnant, but it was far from an act of indiscriminate violence—more like state-sponsored contract killing. But by then the word had acquired a kind of talismanic force—as if refusing to describe something as terrorism was the next thing to apologizing for it.

By the 1990s, people were crying terrorism whenever they discerned an attempt at intimidation or disruption. Hackers who concocted computer viruses were cyberterrorists, cult leaders were psychological terrorists. Software companies accused Microsoft of terrorism in its efforts to maintain its Windows monopoly, and Microsoft accused Apple Computer of "patent terrorism" after the companies got into a dispute over intellectual property. And when photographer Spencer Tunick got thirty people to lie down naked for a picture in front of the United Nations Building in New York, a critic described the piece as "artistic terrorism at its best."

With that kind of freewheeling precedent, it probably shouldn't have been surprising that the anti-terrorism bill passed by Congress defined terrorism very broadly, so that a "terrorist offense" could include anything from hijacking an airplane to injuring government property, breaking into a government computer for any reason, or hitting the secretary of agriculture with a pie. Civil libertarians are concerned that the notion of "terrorism" could become an all-purpose pretext, the way "racketeering" did after the passage of the RICO Act in the 1970s.

That would be a linguistic misfortune, too. Granted, it's natural to appropriate the language of violence when we want to dramatize our zeal or outrage—we make war on poverty, we skirmish over policy, and we cry bloody murder when a hotel misplaces our reservations. But when things happen that merit the full force of our outrage, a legacy of careless usage can leave us at a loss for words.

It May Be Banal but It's Bad News

It may be just a sign of how sheltered my life has been, but I
don't think I've ever known a person who was genuinely evil. I
did know an evil cat once. But that makes my point—evil isn't
something we ascribe to things in the familiar circle of our own
experience. Evil has to be unfathomable, or it isn't evil. And cats
are very good at being unfathomable, whereas dogs always wear
their motivations on their haunches—dogs can't be truly evil,
only mean.

That's why we don't call people evil unless they seem to have
no rational motive for what they do apart from a malignant pleasure in causing pain. The modern paradigm of evil is somebody
like Ted Kaczynski, holed up in a Montana cabin building terror
bombs and torturing his neighbor's dogs. We don't usually use
the word for miscreants who have motives we think we can
understand, like lust and avarice. Kenneth Lay and his fellow
Enron brigands may be a bunch of crooks and liars, but most
people wouldn't call them evil.

It's odd that we should say the love of money is the root of all
evil, since we tend to assume that truly evil people aren't motivated by greed alone. But then when that verse was inserted in

the King James Bible, *evil* had a much broader meaning. The word could refer to just about anything that was wrong, harmful, wretched, disagreeable, or merely unfortunate—the sense the word still has in phrases like "the lesser of two evils." Or it could mean unsatisfactory or just defective—you could complain about an evil meal or evil workmanship. We may think of *evil* as a biblical word, but its meaning is a lot narrower for us than it is in the King James Bible itself—and narrower than traditional theologians would have understood it.

By now, evil has become such a recondite notion that there are only a handful of modern contexts in which we use the word at all. There's Nazi Germany, the model for evil in our time, particularly after Hannah Arendt coined the phrase "the banality of evil" to describe Adolf Eichmann's plodding bureaucratic mind. There are the morally tidy worlds of comic books and James Bond stories, or of gothic movies like *The Exorcist* and *The Omen*, where villainy is rendered with over-the-top campiness—I think of Richard Burton in *The Exorcist II* saying, "We are in the presence of ee-vill."

Those echoes can be hard to escape, even when someone's trying to use the word in deadly earnest. President Bush has done everything he can to tie the word to bin Laden, to the point where he uses "the evil one" as a kind of pronoun. But if the label sticks, it's because bin Laden is a creepy and decidedly unfathomable character who could easily have played the villain in a James Bond movie—or, for those with longer memories, in a Flash Gordon serial, where those orientalist stereotypes were first concocted for the screen.

You can hear the same campy resonances in the phrase "axis of evil" that Bush used in his State of the Union speech. White

House spokesman Ari Fleischer said afterward that Bush didn't intend any literal comparison to the Axis powers in World War II. As he put it, the allusion was "more rhetorical than historical." That's a bit hard to swallow, but it doesn't really matter. No one was liable to confuse Iraq, Iran, and North Korea with the wartime Axis, not just because they're far from allies—two of them can't stand each other, and the third doesn't talk to anybody at all—but because for most listeners "axis of evil" doesn't evoke Churchillian echoes so much as a league of comic-book supervillains.

You can see why Bush finds "evil" a convenient epithet, particularly if he's indifferent to how it sounds in the ears of our allies. It's a corrective for the excesses of moral relativism, it cleaves neatly between us and them, and it simplifies the business of explaining why we fight—and no less important, why they do.

But as various commentators have observed, an absolute term like *evil* can be hard to square with the gradations and relativities that foreign policy is built around. That might not be much of an issue in the case of bin Laden himself, but it's already pushing things for Bush to talk about al Qaeda's "evil weapons," which begs the question of which weapons would be the virtuous ones. And once you try to extend the term, you get into a situation where Colin Powell and Madeleine Albright are having public disagreements over whether the North Koreans should be classified as evil as opposed to merely reprehensible, in which case it's all right to break bread with them. In the end, Bush would have done better to stick with the more familiar label "rogue states." It's hard to imagine a million Iranians taking to the streets in protest because someone has called them rogues.

Even so, the Administration seems bent on pursuing a strategy of *evil*-creep. Bush used the word five times in the State of the Union message and ten times in a speech the following day. And speaking recently in Winston-Salem, North Carolina, he expanded the forces arrayed against the war on evil to include parts of his domestic program, like the AmeriCorps volunteer initiatives. "If you want to fight evil," he said, "we've figured out a way to do so militarily. But at home, you fight evil...by doing something to help somebody."

Nobody's about to question the moral value of home-building and literacy tutoring, but that isn't what we generally have in mind when we talk about fighting evil—illiteracy may be deplorable, but it's a stretch to pin it on Satan. It all has the effect of turning "the war on evil" into routine political rhetoric, and in the course of things that phrase will go the way of other slogans, like "a kinder, gentler nation" and "compassionate conservatism." At that point we can hand the word back to the theologians, only slightly the worse for wear.

Going Nucular

There are two kinds of linguistic missteps, the typos and the thinkos. Typos are the processing glitches that intercede between a thought and its expression. They can make you look foolish, but they aren't really the signs of an intellectual or ethical deficiency, the way thinkos are. It's the difference between a sentence that expresses an idea badly and a sentence that expresses a bad idea.

People don't pay much attention to that distinction when they take after the missteps and malaprops of presidents and other political figures. Maybe it's just because I'm not much of a speller myself, but I've always felt that Dan Quayle got a bum rap over his inability to spell *potatoes*—I mean, there are people who can spell and people who can't, and God doesn't seem to have paid much attention to other cognitive capacities in spreading that gift around. And while critics were always making fun of Eisenhower's woolly language, it wasn't really a sign of woolly thinking—most people realized that he was an astute politician, and he could write lucid prose when he felt like it. Ditto former President Bush: He may have had difficulty speaking complete sentences, but that didn't mean that he wasn't thinking complete thoughts.

Fresh Air Commentary, October 2, 2002

No president has taken more flak over his language than George W. Bush—not Eisenhower, not even Harding. That's understandable enough; Bush's malaprops can make him sound like someone who learned the language over a bad cell-phone connection. "My education message will resignate among all parents"; "A tax cut is really one of the anecdotes to coming out of an economic illness."

The columnists and late-night talk-show monologists usually take those errors as the occasions for mirth, rather than concern, the linguistic equivalents of Gerald Ford's pratfalls. Bush himself encouraged that interpretation with those Letterman and *Saturday Night Live* appearances during the campaign, when he made fun of his inability to pronounce *subliminal* and said he was "ambilavant" about appearing on the show. It was a shrewd maneuver, as Mark Crispin Miller pointed out in his recent book *The Bush Dyslexicon*, a penetrating look at Bush and his language. The self-mockery took the edge off the criticisms by painting Bush as just another irrepressible word-mangler, sort of a Yalie Casey Stengel.

But it isn't always easy to tell whether an error is a typo or a thinko. Take the pronunciation of *nuclear* as "nucular." That one has been getting on people's nerves ever since Eisenhower made the mispronunciation famous in the 1950s. In Woody Allen's 1989 film *Crimes and Misdemeanors*, the Mia Farrow character says she could never fall for any man who says "nucular." That would have ruled out not just Dubya, but Bill Clinton, who said the word right only about half the time. (President Carter had his own way of saying the word, as "newkeeuh," but that probably had more to do with his Georgia accent than his ignorance of English spelling.)

On the face of things, "nucular" is a typo par excellence. People sometimes talk about Bush "stumbling" over the word, as if this were the same kind of articulatory problem that turns *February* into "febyooary." But *nuclear* isn't a hard word to pronounce the way *February* is—try saying each of them three times fast. Phonetically, in fact, *nuclear* is pretty much the same as *likelier*, and nobody ever says "The first outcome was likulier than the second." That "nucular" pronunciation is really what linguists call a folk etymology, where the unfamiliar word *nuclear* is treated as if it had the same suffix as words like *molecular* and *particular*. It's the same process that turns *lackadaisical* into "laxadaisical" and *chaise longue* into *chaise lounge*.

That accounts for Eisenhower's mispronunciation of *nuclear*, back in a time when the word was a new addition to ordinary people's vocabularies. And it's why Homer Simpson says it as "nucular" even today. But it doesn't explain why you still hear "nucular" from people like politicians, military people, and weapons specialists, most of whom obviously know better and have been reminded repeatedly what the correct pronunciation is. I have an old college friend who says the word that way, someone who works as an atomic weapons wallah at a federal agency. I asked him once if anybody ever corrected him on it, and he said, "Well, sometimes the physicists I talk to get shirty about it. But they know what I'm talking about." Then out of curiosity I asked him if he ever talked about "nucular families." "Of course not," he said, "I only say 'nucular' when I'm talking about nukes."

In the mouths of those people, "nucular" is a choice, not an inadvertent mistake—a thinko, not a typo. Maybe it appeals to them to refer to the weapons in what seems like a folksy and familiar way, or maybe it's a question of asserting their authority—

"We're the ones with our fingers on the button, and we'll pronounce the word however we damn well please."

But which of these stories explains why Bush says "nucular"? Most people seem to assume he's just one of those people who don't know any better. But that's hard to credit. After all, Bush didn't have to learn the word *nuclear* in middle age, the way Eisenhower did. He must have heard it said correctly thousands of times when he was growing up—not just at Andover, Yale, and Harvard, but from his own father, who never seems to have had any trouble with the word. But if Bush's "nucular" is a deliberate choice, is it something he picked up from the Pentagon wise guys? Or is it a faux-bubba pronunciation, the sort of thing he might have started doing at Andover or Yale, by way of playing the Texan to all those earnest Eastern dweebs?

Actually, there would be an easy way to tell—just see how Bush pronounces *nuclear* in phrases like *nuclear family* and *nuclear medicine*. If he says "nucular" all the time, then it's most likely a faux-bubba thing. But if he only says "nucular" for weapons, it's probably a bit of borrowed Pentagon swagger. I'll be keeping my ears peeled.

Appease Porridge Hot

The English philosopher Peter Strawson talked about expressions that had "grown capital letters"—descriptions like *The Cold War*, *The Flood*, or *The Sultan of Swat*, which have turned into quasi-proper names. But sometimes an expression gets attached to a particular event without actually becoming a name for it—it's more like picking up a piece of dirt that it can't scrape off its shoes. *Stonewalling* for example—it isn't a proper name, but it always evokes the Nixon administration's response to Watergate. Ditto *isolationism* or *death squad* or *partition*—they're each linked to a particular historical moment.

Or take *appeasement*. Whenever it's pronounced, the word conjures up the memory of Prime Minister Neville Chamberlain standing on the steps of 10 Downing Street on his return from the Munich conference in September 1938, after he had handed over the Czech Sudetenland to Hitler. "It is peace for our time," he told the press. "Go home and get a nice quiet sleep."

That moment had a number of far-reaching consequences—I mean, over and above bringing the world a step closer to a catastrophic war. It sealed the political downfall of Chamberlain, and it revived the faded fortunes of Winston Churchill, who had

Fresh Air Commentary, February 19, 2003

opposed the Munich decision as "complete surrender . . . to the Nazi threat of force." And it permanently changed the meaning of the word *appeasement* itself.

Before Munich, *appeasement* didn't have the dishonorable connotations it does for us. *Appease* still carried the echoes of the root sense of *peace*, and its meaning was simply "conciliate" or "pacify"—this was before *pacification* got its feet muddy, too. That's the sense the word has in the verse from the Book of Proverbs: "He that is slow to anger appeaseth strife." In fact Churchill himself recommended a policy of "prudence and appeasement" towards the Turks when they went to war with the Greeks in 1919. And Roosevelt described Mussolini's conquest of Ethiopia in 1936 as an "integral measure for world appeasement." That's the meaning that Chamberlain had in mind when he talked about a policy of appeasement—the idea was not to capitulate to dictators but to ensure the peace while Britan had time to re-arm, after the defense cuts that Churchill presided over when he was the defence minister in the 1920s. In retrospect, the appeasement policy may have been disastrously short-sighted, but it wasn't intended to be pusillanimous—and in fact Chamberlain had few illusions about Hitler's intentions.

But no politician since then has been able to talk about appeasement in an approving way. After Munich, the word could only suggest a cowardly capitulation to the demands of tyrants in the hope that they'll refrain from further aggression. That's why the word is so inflammatory when it's used to describe opponents of the Administration's Iraq policy. I've been hearing more and more of this—I counted over eighty uses of "appeasement" in the press last month in stories about Iraq in major papers in January 2003, three times as many as in the month before. And the other day Condoleezza Rice gave official sanction to the label on *Meet the Press*, when she likened the Security Council's actions to the appeasement of Hitler in the 1930s.

That comparison obviously isn't designed to bring any allies around; it's strictly for the benefit of the Administration's own troops. It's part of a blitzkrieg aimed at seizing the moral high ground, even if you have to roll over history and etymology in the process. Whatever your view of the French and German position on Saddam Hussein, after all, it isn't remotely comparable to the attitude that Chamberlain is supposed to have taken towards Hitler—"Let's give him what he wants and maybe he'll leave us alone."

In fact, neither Churchill nor any other critic of Chamberlain's appeasement policy ever argued for a pre-emptive strike on Germany. They simply supported what people would now describe as deterrence and containment, pretty much as the French and Germans are doing now. With the wisdom of hindsight, of course, you could argue that even that would have been an inadequate response to the threat of Hitler—if we were rewriting history, we'd have had Britain and France make an alliance with Stalin to go after Germany then and there. And if you were of a mind to, you could say that the Security Council is making the same mistake now that Churchill made in 1938—that is, if you're willing to argue that Saddam Hussein represents the same threat to world security that Hitler did back then.

But one way or the other, that isn't a conversation that anybody's about to launch, at least outside of history department common rooms. It's hard to imagine the Administration comparing the Security Council to Churchill, not when the adjective *Churchillian* has become an epithet that is as uncritically laudatory as *appeasement* is derogatory.

The anthropologist Claude Lévi-Strauss once said that every

important event lives two lives, one as history and one as myth. Political language plays a big part in that transformation—it turns the lessons of history into a set of Cliffs Notes. All that complicated historical footage reduces to a couple of stills—Churchill as the resolute foe of bullies, glaring over his cigar; Chamberlain as the archetypal Euroweenie, with his striped pants, high collar, umbrella, and drooping moustache. And Munich itself has become one of those words like Waterloo, Verdun, and Pearl Harbor—names that have seceded from the flesh-and-blood past and taken up a life of their own as moral fables in the popular imagination. If some words have grown capital letters and become proper names, *Munich* and the rest are proper names that politics has turned into common nouns.

The Second Casualty

"The first casualty when war comes is truth." With due respect to Hiram Johnson, the Progressive senator who made that famous remark in 1917, the first casualty of war is less often the truth itself than the way we tell it. Coloring the facts is usually more convenient than falsifying them.

The modern language of war emerged in the Victorian age, when military planners first became concerned about public opinion. One linguistic casualty of that period was *casualty* itself, a word for an accidental loss that became a euphemism for dead and wounded around the time of the Crimean War, the conflict that gave birth to the war correspondent.

By World War I, the modern language of warfare was in its full euphemistic glory. The mutinies among French troops in 1917 were described in dispatches as "acts of collective indiscipline," and the writers of the daily communiqués from the Western Front were instructed to use the phrase "brisk fighting" to describe any action in which more than 50 percent of a company was killed or wounded.

What's notable about the latest war isn't the toll it has taken on language—all wars do that—but the obsessive attention we've paid to the matter. There has never been an age that was so self-conscious about the way it talked about war. Barely two weeks into the Iraq conflict, more than a dozen articles had appeared in major newspapers speculating about what its effects on the language would be, as if that would reveal to us what story we would wind up telling about it.

In part, that is simply a reaction to the jumble of images and reports we've been subjected to, and of the need to make sense of them. Last week, Defense Secretary Rumsfeld complained that the abruptly shifting impressions of the war's progress were due to viewers seeing "every second another slice of what's actually happening over there." He waxed nostalgic for World War II newsreels that wrapped the week's war highlights in a stirring narrative.

Rumsfeld's wistfulness is understandable. True, domestic support for World War II was never as solid or uncritical as we like to imagine—as late as 1944, almost 40 percent of Americans said they favored a negotiated peace with the Germans. But there's no trace of those doubts in the language the war left us with, or in the artless enthusiasm of those newsreels: "Then, by light of the moon, a thousand mighty bombing planes take off, flying to their marks and releasing their fatal loads."

That was the tail end of a purple thread that ran back to those Crimean dispatches about gallant British troops pouring fire on the terrible enemy. The effusive metaphors of the newsreels were already shopworn in 1969, when Rumsfeld joined Nixon's cabinet, and war reports from Vietnam had to be tailored to an increasingly skeptical and knowing public.

Today, no journalist would hazard a reference to mighty bombers dropping fatal loads. Embedded reporters produce embedded language, the metallic clatter of modern military lingo: acronyms like TLAMs, RPGs and MREs; catchphrases like "asymmetric warfare," "emerging targets" and "catastrophic success"—the last not an oxymoron, but an irresistibly perverse phrase for a sudden acceleration of good fortune.

I prefer that jargon to the mighty bombers. It's truer to the nature of modern warfare, and it sometimes rises to a kind of brutalist poetry, as in, "Their units have been significantly degraded or attrited." (Milton would have recognized *attrited* as the past tense of *attrite*, meaning "grind away"; the verb has merely been lying low for 300 years.)

When it comes to penetrating the fog of battle, though, the words are rarely new. They're recycled phrases drawn from earlier wars and conflicts, trailing vague clouds of glory or obloquy, and smoothed by the selectivity of historical memory. "Liberation" evokes the image of the soldiers on American tanks sweeping up pretty demoiselles in their arms as they rolled through Normandy, not the guerrilla wars of national liberation that troubled American foreign policy for much of the Cold War.

President Bush's father would probably have thought twice before talking about Saddam Hussein's "death squads," lest the phrase recall the Guatemalan and Salvadorean regimes that the Reagan administration supported when he was vice president. His son can use the words in the confidence that time has attrited their historical resonances. And a decade or so ago, Ari Fleischer's assurance that "slowly but surely the hearts and minds of the Iraqi people are being won" would still have evoked disconcerting memories. But Fleischer was barely fifteen years old when Peter Davis's anti-Vietnam War documentary *Hearts and Minds* won an Oscar in 1975. Even "shock and awe" sounds vaguely familiar, like the name of some heavy-metal tour from the early '90s.

The ambient war-speak strikes your consciousness as an odd jumble, patched together from the half-remembered motifs of old Chuck Norris movies and documentaries from the History Channel, and tweaked from hour to hour to accommodate the latest developments. It's pastiche, the genre that the literary critic Fredric Jameson described as a statue with blind eyes; the language doesn't so much relate as reverberate.

With words as vague as these, truth is less a casualty than an irrelevancy. Is this really a liberation? Compared to what? It's always a mug's game trying to pin down the meanings of these labels. ("That depends on what the meaning of *cakewalk* is.") And in any case, the language doesn't really work at the level of meaning. Asking whether people believe the words is like asking whether they believe the drum tattoo that MSNBC plays as the screen fades to commercial breaks, under the names of soldiers who have made "the ultimate sacrifice."

There's a paradox in the way we think about political language: The wiser we are to its tricks, the more we worry about its manipulative power—not over ourselves, but over the innocents who are still stirred by words like *mighty*. There aren't many linguistic innocents left in America, of course; 1984 is probably the only novel that all of my students have read. But we tell ourselves that language still has power over those who haven't had our advantages. The Bush administration dropped its references to "fedayeen" last week when it was reminded that the word has heroic connotations in the Arabic-speaking world, and began to refer to the militia fighters as "terrorists" or "thugs" instead. Not that Americans need those hints, an official explained, but "in other parts of the world, labeling helps to put it in perspective."

World War II contributed hundreds of words to our vocabulary. But the language of recent wars has faded very rapidly, like the memories of our reasons for fighting them. Within a short time, "shock and awe" will be a Trivial Pursuit item like "mother of all battles" from the 1991 Persian Gulf war. War language does a different kind of work now. What remains with us isn't the words, but the tunes they're meant to bring to mind. It's like that corny tattoo on MSNBC: You see right through it, and it raises a shiver anyway.

Naming of Foreign Parts

To a lot of its critics, the Administration's miscalculations in its Mideast policy are summed up in a single pronunciation: "Eye-rack." Nicholas Kristof wrote recently in *The New York Times* that "Arabs flinch each time American officials torture pronunciations of the names of Iraqi cities and, worse, the country itself.... The Bush administration might at least remind officials that we are not invading Eye-rack, but Ee-rack."

But if people in Amman, Cairo, and Riyadh are flinching as they watch the TV news nowadays, I doubt if it has much to do with the way American politicians and journalists are struggling with the intricacies of Arabic phonology—no more than the current wave of anti-French feeling owes anything to Jacques Chirac's pronunciation of our president's first name as "zhorrrzh."

Anyway, however hard Americans try to approximate the pronunciations of Arabic names, what comes out of our mouths is going to be pretty remote from the real thing to Arab ears. If you were really going to get the name of the country right, you'd say something like "EE-rawq," with that guttural *q* that doesn't have any English equivalent. And you'd start it with an "ayn," an *h*-like sound that's pronounced even farther back in the throat.

"BAGGH-ded," "KurbeLEH," "BASS-rah." That's what Arabic speakers tell me, but it's a fool's errand for Americans to try to do those names justice. The prudent course is to make a yeoman effort at approximating foreign names with the limited phonetic resources that English makes available. Going further than that is almost always a sign of dubious ulterior motives. There are those Spanish pronunciations that are supposed to demonstrate solidarity with the locals, like "NeecaRAWWa" and "CoLOHMMbia." Or there are the sprezzatura pronunciations of the classical music announcers, who linger on the double *t* of Pavarotti and the *th*-sound of PlaTHido Domingo.

And then there are the trench-coat pronunciations that you hear from journalists who want to intimate that they've spent a long time, as they say, on the ground. I think of the way Daniel Schorr used to talk about MikhILE GorbaTCHOFF, with the easy familiarity of an old Kremlin hand. There's a hint of this in the way journalists have taken up saying "gutter" for the country that the uninitiated refer to as "katt-AR." Actually it isn't at all clear that the locals would recognize the journalists' "gutter" as a version of what they pronounce as something like "QAW-tar." (The nation's embassy answers the phone as "Embassy of katt-AR," in any case.) But then these attempts at phonetic correctness are really intended for domestic consumption.

There's a domestic note in those criticisms of the pronunciation "eye-rack," too. A lot of people see the pronunciation as a symptom of redneck ignorance—columnists have suggested that it's somehow tied to Americans' general fuzziness about geographical detail and our insensitivity to the complexities of world politics. As a columnist for the Baltimore *Sun* wrote not long ago, "If you can't pronounce it, don't try to invade it."

But the idea that "eye-rack" is incorrect is mostly a sign of our own linguistic prejudices. The pronunciation has two things working against it. The first syllable fits in with that pattern of saying certain foreign words with a long vowel—not just "eye-rack" and "eye-ran," but words like "ay-rab" and "eye-talian," pronunciations that educated people tend to associate with red-state yahoos. And then there's the flat-fronted vowel of the second syllable—"rack" instead of "rock." That runs afoul of the principle that the letter *a* in foreign names should always be pronounced as "ah." That has become an article of faith among well-traveled Americans, to the point where "milahn" or "milano" have replaced the time-honored "milann."

Hearing people ridicule ordinary Americans who say "eye-rack" can be like listening to American expatriates sneering at the tourists in line at the Louvre or the Coliseum. But it's something else again when you hear that pronunciation coming from Administration officials who don't come by it natively. In their mouths, it smacks of calculated folksiness, as if to tweak all those fastidious internationalists—we can go it alone phonetically, too. It has gotten to the point where you can tell people's position on the role the United Nations should play in the reconstruction of Iraq just by listening to the way they say the name.

For the time being, "ee-rock" would seem to be the more judicious pronunciation, at least until we're certain that when the dust clears, we won't need any assistance in writing the gazetteers for this part of the world. But I'm not really bothered hearing journalists and politicians make a hash out of those other exotic Arabic placenames. I've been listening occasionally to French news broadcasts over the Internet, and their announcers do a much better job with Arabic names, no doubt because they have had a couple of hundred years of embedding in the Arabic-speaking world. It's an impressive phonetic accomplishment, but you hope we don't get to that point ourselves.

The Syntax of Resistance

Sometimes a social change can announce itself in the dropping of a preposition. It used to be that when you used the verb *protest* to mean "object to" you had to add *against*—"She protested against her mistreatment." Then in the early years of the twentieth century, Americans began to say things like "He protested the government's policy."

As it happens, it was around the time that people started using *protest* with a direct object that they also started to think of protest as a kind of direct political action aimed at mobilizing public opinion against a particular policy. That's when phrases like "protest demonstration," "protest strike," and "protest movement" began to appear.

Or take "protest march." I had always assumed that the phrase originated with the ban-the-bomb movement of the 1950s—the *Oxford English Dictionary* gives the first citation of the word from 1959. But in fact it goes back much further than that; it was used in 1913 to describe a march that Gandhi organized to protest the restrictions that had been imposed on the Indian population of South Africa, in the first massive civil disobedience campaign. Over the following decades, *protest* would be intimately linked with

Fresh Air Commentary, March 11, 2003

those new techniques of political resistance. By the 1930s, people were using phrases like "the literature of protest" and "social protest" to suggest the whole range of progressive agitation.

But it wasn't until the sixties that the notion of protest entered the mainstream of the American vocabulary. That was the moment when songs with political messages began to make their way out of the coffee houses and hootenannies and onto the airwaves. For some people, "protest music" evokes the folk-inspired topical songs of Pete Seeger, Joan Baez, Phil Ochs, Country Joe McDonald, and the early Dylan. But by the mid-sixties people were using the phrase for songs like *Blowin' in the Wind* and Barry McGuire's 1965 *Eve of Destruction*, which was the first protest song to become a number one hit. *Eve of Destruction*'s lyrics were mostly a generic plea for peace and understanding, a pretty far cry from Phil Ochs's *The War Is Over* or the Fugs's *Kill for Peace*. Even so, a lot of AM stations refused to play the song, and conservatives complained to the FCC that the song violated the equal time provision, back before they learned they could live nicely without it.

By then, people had begun to use the noun *protest* as short-hand for a clamorous rally. That gave rise to the word *PROtester* in place of the older form *proTESTer*, which was derived from the verb. The shift in stress corresponded to a difference in emphasis. *ProTESTer* suggests an individual with a specific beef in mind, whereas when you hear *PROtester* you think of a group of angry people kicking up a row. The new noun gave rise to a new way of pronouncing the verb, as well. By now, there's a marked semantic difference between saying "The lady doth proTEST too much" and "The lady doth PROtest too much"—the latter sounds like Bill O'Reilly talking about Janeane Garofalo.

By the time the Vietnam War ended, the notion of "protests" was losing its connection with the old tradition of social protest. There's a revealing use of the word in the 1982 film *First Blood*, the first and by far the best of the Rambo movies. It comes when Rambo is describing his return from Vietnam: "And I come back to the world and I see all those maggots at the airport, protesting me, spitting. Calling me baby killer. . . . Who are they to protest me?" Granted, Rambo was supposed to be a little unhinged, but by then a lot of people wouldn't have seen anything odd in the notion of a "protest" aimed at individual soldiers—it was becoming just another name for a demonstration.

That's apparently all the word means to some people now, as protests are back in the streets. The other day I saw the influential libertarian-conservative blogger Glenn Reynolds referring to "the growing pro-war protest movement." That took me aback, but when I hunted around, I found a number of other conservatives using the word that way. The Web site of the Young Americans for Freedom boasts about the pro-war protests that the group organized at the University of Michigan. Even the press is starting to pick this up—an article in the Seattle *Times* last week talked about the "protestors" at a pro-Bush demonstration who were waving signs saying "Support Our Troops."

There's a certain disingenuousness in those uses of *protest*. I don't mean that the word can only be used for manifestations by the left. There's nothing odd in talking about a conservative campus group holding a protest over the university president's support of affirmative action or staging a protest demonstration outside CNN headquarters to protest media bias. That may not exactly conjure up the old notion of Protest with a capital P, but it's clearly a form of resistance to the established order.

But it sounds a little odd to talk about a protest in support of a war that's about to be initiated by the Administration in power. Maybe that's just semantic sloppiness, as if "protesting" nowadays were just a question of getting together to yell slogans—why should the other side have all the fun? Or maybe it's a strategic blurring of historical memory. It's hard to keep this stuff straight in an age when the oldies stations are apt to play Barry McGuire's *Eve of Destruction* back-to-back with Barry Sadler's *Ballad of the Green Berets*, which was a number one hit a few months later.

But you'd hope that *protest* would retain some of the sense of resistance that it acquired at the beginning of the last century. Up to now, after all, protest has been the only form of political action that power can't engage in.

A Couple of Words for Nothing Left to Lose

What exactly are we fighting for? In his speech to the nation explaining America's goals, President Bush said we were fighting to "defend our freedom" and "bring freedom to others." Nowadays, Americans always go to war under the banner of freedom, ours or theirs: Operation Iraqi Freedom follows Operation Enduring Freedom in Afghanistan.

There was a time when the campaign would have been fought in the name of liberty. We had a reminder of that when the efforts to rebaptize french fries as "freedom fries" led commentators to recall the First World War renamings of sauerkraut as "liberty cabbage" and dachshunds as "liberty dogs," in an earlier episode of jingoistic fatuity. The choice of "freedom fries" may have owed something to alliteration, but *liberty* was much more prominent in the early-twentieth-century patriotic lexicon than it is now. Americans wore liberty buttons, bought liberty bonds, and planted liberty gardens, while our factories turned out liberty trucks and the liberty engine, designed to power the DeHavilland bombers built in the U.S.

If the War To End War were being refought today, it's a safe bet that we would be talking about freedom bonds and freedom trucks. For that matter, a modern patriot who was writing the Pledge of Allegiance from scratch would probably conclude it "with freedom and justice for all."

This shift from *liberty* to *freedom* is a subtle one, which few other languages would even be able to express. The French national motto is usually translated as "Liberty, equality, fraternity," but *liberté* could as easily be translated as "freedom." And even in English, the words can sometimes seem to be equivalent. The philosopher Isaiah Berlin used them more or less interchangeably in his influential essay "Two Concepts of Liberty," and so did the historian Eric Foner in his *The Story of American Freedom*, which traces the evolution of the concept from Colonial times. Sometimes, in fact, the words are incanted in the same breath—"The issue is freedom and liberty," President Bush said a few days before the war began. Or as the Grateful Dead put it, "Ooo, freedom/ Ooo, liberty/ Ooo, leave me alone."

But English hasn't taken the trouble to retain all those pairs of Anglo-Saxon and Latin near-synonyms just so its thesauruses could be heftier. There's a difference between friendship and amity, or a paternal manner and a fatherly one. And *liberty* and *freedom* have distinct meanings, too, even if it isn't easy to pin them down. As the political theorist Hanna Fenichel Pitkin has observed, liberty implies a system of rules, a "network of restraint and order," which is why the word is closely associated with political life. *Freedom* has a more general meaning, which ranges from an opposition to slavery to the absence of psychological or personal encumbrances—no one would describe *liberty* as another name for nothing left to lose.

But the two words have been continually redefined over the centuries, as Americans contested the basic notion of what it means to be free. For the founders of the nation, liberty was the fundamental American value. That was a legacy of the conception of "English liberty," with which Britons proudly distinguished themselves from the slavish peoples of the Continent who were unprotected from the arbitrary power of the state. Echoing John Locke, the Declaration of Independence speaks of "life, liberty and the pursuit of happiness"; the text doesn't mention freedom at all. It was liberty that Patrick Henry declared himself willing to die for, and liberty that the ringing bell in Philadelphia proclaimed on July 8, 1776.

Liberty remained the dominant patriotic theme for the following 150 years. True, freedom played an important role, particularly in the debates over slavery. Lincoln's Gettysburg Address began by invoking a nation "conceived in liberty," but went on to resolve that it should have a "new birth of freedom." But *freedom* didn't really come into its own until the New Deal period, when the defining American values were augmented to include the economic and social justice that permitted people free development as human beings. Of Roosevelt's Four Freedoms—of speech, of religion, from want, and from fear—only the first two might have been expressed using *liberty*.

The civil rights movement made "freedom now" its rallying cry. Martin Luther King Jr. used *freedom* nineteen times in his "I Have a Dream" speech, and *liberty* only twice. Feminists extended freedom to cover reproductive rights, while Timothy Leary spoke of the "fifth freedom . . . the freedom to expand your own consciousness."

But as Eric Foner has observed, freedom is too central in the American consciousness to remain the property of one political side. The conservative reclaiming of the word began during the

Cold War, when it was expanded to include the benefits of free markets and the consumer choices they provided. Then, too, freedom was a conveniently vague label used to describe free-world allies like Franco's Spain, whose commitment to liberty was questionable.

No one understood better than Ronald Reagan the power that *freedom* had acquired. His second Inaugural Address mentioned freedom fourteen times and liberty only once. But in the mouth of Reagan and other conservatives, *freedom* conveyed what Isaiah Berlin called its negative sense, an absence of constraints on markets and individual action. Reagan's program of "economic freedom" included deregulation, tax cuts, and a weakening of unions, which earlier conservatives had championed in the name of the "liberty of employers."

The invocation of freedom became as reflexive for the right as it had been for New Deal Democrats and those in the civil rights movement. Opponents of civil rights legislation appealed to "freedom of association," and in 1981, Pat Robertson founded the Freedom Council to advance a Christian Conservative program. On the National Rifle Association's Web site, *freedom* is three times as frequent as *liberty*.

As the expanding use of *freedom* makes every policy and program a part of the national mission, *liberty* has receded from the patriotic vocabulary. If we still venerate the word now, it's less as a rallying cry than as a stand-in for the legalistic niceties that the founders took such trouble over. That's why the word still comes up when the conversation turns to the domestic war on terrorism, whether in the expression "civil liberties" or standing alone.

Lately, Bush administration figures have been trying to wrest the word *liberty* from the critics of their homeland security measures. When a special appeals court upheld the wiretap provisions of the USA Patriot Act a few months ago, Attorney General John Ashcroft called the decision "a victory for liberty, safety, and the security of the American people." And Homeland Security Secretary Tom Ridge announced Operation Liberty Shield, which will step up surveillance of those suspected of terrorist ties and authorize indefinite detention of asylum-seekers from certain nations.

Even so, a lot of people still hold that liberty and safety, like guns and butter, are notions that are more appropriately opposed than conjoined. They're mindful of Benjamin Franklin's warning that "they that can give up essential liberty to obtain a little temporary safety deserve neither liberty nor safety."

Right now, "Iraqi Freedom" conveys something more basic than "American freedom" suggests—it is simply emancipation from tyranny, not a choice of SUVs or an end to double taxation of dividends. The Iraqis may someday enjoy those more advanced varieties of freedom. Ultimately, they may even enjoy liberty. But that will require more time, and as we have had ample opportunity to learn, eternal vigilance.

The Gallic Subject

Reading through recent commentaries on European reactions to the Administration's line on Iraq, I kept running into the adjective *Gallic*—"the great dismal fog of Gallic anti-Americanism"; "the duplicities of Gallic diplomacy"; "Gallic intransigence." An op-ed piece in the *Los Angeles Times* had French foreign minister Dominique de Villepin displaying a "Gallic insouciance" to Colin Powell's presentation before the Security Council, and at least three other columns described the French reaction to the speech as a "Gallic shrug"—one of them, by William Safire, presciently appearing before the speech had actually been made.

It's an odd word, one of a handful of fanciful adjectives like *Hibernian* for the Irish, *Caledonian* for the Scots, and *Teutonic* for the Germans, which journalists keep handy to conjure up a familiar national stereotype. The cluster of nouns that gravitate towards *Gallic* suggests the mix of infatuation and exasperation that the French always evoke for American readers. Phrases like "Gallic charm" and "Gallic flair" are paired with "Gallic rudeness" and "Gallic arrogance," and of course those inevitable "Gallic shrugs," a phrase that turns up almost 700 times in the Nexis major newspaper database. And then there's "Gallic logic,"

Fresh Air Commentary, February 12, 2003

a term usually preceded by "impeccable." (The French are the only people we credit with having a national logic of their own.)

But one way or the other, *Gallic* always implies the traits of character—you don't see people talking about "Gallic aircraft carriers" or "Gallic pharmaceutical companies." According to Edward Knox, a professor at Middlebury College who has studied the way France is reported in the American press, *Gallic* isn't really a synonym for French at all—it's more like a shorthand for "the French are at it again."

Gallic is just one of the vocabulary items that journalists have consecrated to the French. In press stories, the French are always "fuming" about something or other, and where other peoples say things, the French sniff them—as in 'We were not informed of the decision,' the minister sniffed." In fact the adjective *sniffy* is another favorite here, and the French are described as snooty even more often than the English are. In the American press, the Frenchman is depicted as a character who's guided by his nose, whereas the German is a character who's led by it.

Journalists have been dining out on these turns of phrase since Mark Twain's time, but it's striking how readily they come up when the French are proving obstinate over American policy. You don't often hear *Teutonic* used in the same way to describe the Germans' reluctance to go along. Not long ago the *London Times* columnist Michael Gove suggested that the Germans' present pacifism grows out of "a historic weakness in the German character" of the same sort that led to Hitlerism—"a tendency among German elites over the past 200 years to invest the ruling ideology of the moment with the quasi-mystical quality of a political religion." But most Americans would see that as a stretch—whatever annoyance they may feel about the German position, they don't feel the need to connect it to Colonel Klink.

One reason why journalists single out the French is just because they can: The French happen to be one of the few European nationalities who don't have an American constituency to look out for their interests. What if the Italians had sided with the French and the Germans in opposing American policy on Iraq? I doubt whether commentators would be bringing up the Italian reputation for military faint-heartedness, in the way Representative Peter King did with the French a few days ago when he suggested that they could go to Baghdad "to instruct the Iraqis in how to surrender." And you can be sure that critics wouldn't be throwing around epithets like *wops* and *dagos* the way they have with *frogs*.

True, the French have an annoying habit of vaunting their sense of cultural superiority to Americans. But the Italians, Germans, and English have exactly the same condescending attitude—though, as with the French, it's usually mixed with a genuine affection for the engaging upstarts of the New World. If there's a difference between the French and the others, it has more to do with an ambivalence about the cachet that French culture has in this country. Often you sense that the animus is directed less at the French than at francophiles—the people the right is quick to describe as the "Chablis and brie set."

It brings to mind the description that Mark Twain gave in *The Innocents Abroad* of the Frenchified American he encountered in Venice who's sporting a rose in his buttonhole and calling Paris "Paree": "Oh, it is pitiable to see him making of himself a thing that is neither male nor female, neither fish, flesh, nor fowl—a poor, miserable, hermaphrodite Frenchman!"

You could hear that same disdain for the American francophile classes in a recent *National Review* piece by the conservative columnist Victor Davis Hanson. As he put it, "heartland Americans . . . far from being deprived yokels, have a clearer appreciation of the quite profound amorality in Europe than anyone in the Ivy League." Still, it was notable that Hanson couldn't get out of that commentary without throwing in an indignant "mon dieu!" Whenever you see the word *Gallic* in a story, it's bucks to beignets it will be followed by a phrase like "tête-à-tête" or "vive la différence" or "je ne sais quoi," just so the writers can make it clear that they aren't deprived yokels themselves. As the critics of the French are always making a point of saying: "You can take my word for it—I've *been* there."

That's why France-bashing is a perennially satisfying exercise—you can take a stick to the decadent European wussiness of your compatriots while at the same time making a show of your own cosmopolitan savoir faire. A pity the French are so prone to Gallic touchiness, or they'd see it all for the tribute it is.

Begin the Régime

There's nothing so powerful as a slogan whose time has come. In 2001 there were a total of nine mentions of the phrase "regime change" in major newspapers; since January of this year there have been more than six hundred. Yet there's nothing new about the notion of regime change itself. I've found the phrase in political science articles from as far back as 1968. And *regime* has suggested impermanence ever since it first entered the English political lexicon just after the French Revolution. That was the mother of all regime changes, and it gave us the phrase *ancien régime*, or "old regime," as a name for the form of government that was about to come to a decisive end.

Regime first entered English as a way of referring to a country's form of government. In that use, it needn't be disparaging—people talk about democratic or parliamentary regimes as easily as about totalitarian regimes. But when we call a government a regime, there's usually a sense that its hold on power is insecure or unsteady, as if you could hear the tumbrils rolling in the distance. We talk about the democratic regimes of Latin America, but not about the democratic regimes of North America or Western Europe—those we just call democracies. As best I can

Fresh Air Commentary, October 21, 2002

tell, the difference between a democratic regime and a democracy is that with the latter you don't have to keep checking in to see who's in charge.

But *regime* has another, more recent use, where it refers to the particular people in power in a country, rather than to its form of government. That's the sense that *regime* has when it's paired with the name of a ruler or a political party, like "the Castro regime" or "the Sandinista regime." Or people sometimes talk about "the Havana regime" or "the Beijing regime," with the implication that the rulers just happen to be squatting in the seat of government. In those cases, *regime* always implies that the government is illegitimate or undemocratic. We don't talk about the Ottawa regime or the Washington regime. And the only people who talk about the "London regime" are Irish nationalists referring to the Unionist government in Belfast, which proves the point.

You can get a sense of just how high a government ranks on the current public enemies list just by seeing how likely the press is to describe it as a regime. When I did those counts on the names of current rulers, Saddam Hussein came in first, and second place was a tie between Castro and the Assads of Syria. Then came Gadhafi, the North Koreans, and the Iranians, with the Chinese and the Saudis trailing well behind.

There's a clear tendency here for the press to use *regime* more for governments that the U.S. has particularly antagonistic relations with. The Castro government is more than twice as likely to be called a regime as the Beijing government is, and the Syrians are six times as likely to get the label as the Saudis or Musharraf are. Still, I can see the journalistic logic to this. The label *regime* implies impermanence, after all, and historically, governments that have gotten on the wrong side of the United States haven't generally proved very stable. In the past, in fact, the press has used *regime* most frequently for leaders that the U.S. was actively trying to topple, like the Sandinistas, Noriega, Milosevic, and the Taliban. The only difference between then and now is that the phrase "regime change" seems to make that principle a matter of official policy.

What makes "regime change" such an inspired slogan is the way it plays on the ambiguity of *regime* itself. Everybody knows what the Administration's supporters have uppermost in their minds when they talk about regime change. Ari Fleischer made that quite clear when he said that regime change in Iraq could be accomplished for the cost of a single bullet. But in the language of diplomacy, "regime change" plays a lot better than a slogan like "let's take out this bozo"; it suggests that what the U.S. is ultimately interested in is replacing the current Iraqi system with something more benign. "Regime change"—you have the picture of a country gleaming with all the appurtenances of a modern democracy: a League of Women Voters, Sunday morning with Tim Russert, attack ads, and hanging chads.

Well, stranger things have happened in the last few decades. But regime change can be an unpredictable business, as liberals like Condorcet and Lafayette discovered at the time of that *ur*-regime change of 1789. In the first flush of revolutionary hope, they coined the phrase *le nouveau régime* to describe the new democratic order that they were building. But the phrase never caught on the way *ancien régime* did, probably because it was quickly overtaken by events. Over the following decades, the French went through a series of dictatorships, despotisms, monarchies, communes, and short-lived republics, throwing the whole region into a turmoil that it took a hundred and fifty years to recover from. It wasn't till eighty years after the fall of the Bastille that the French finally stopped lurching from one regime to the next and settled into a more-or-less stable democratic system that nobody was tempted to describe as a regime in the first place. It's easier to get rid of regimes than to create a world where we don't actually have to use the word.

We'll Always Have Kirkuk

"We did not . . . defeat a brutal dictator and liberate 25 million people only to retreat before a band of thugs and assassins." That was President Bush addressing troops in Baghdad during his holiday drop-in, picking two terms from the long list of epithets for the bad guys in Iraq.

A CBS News report last week used five different names in the space of a couple of paragraphs. It was headed "Series of Strikes on Iraq Rebels," and it went on to say, "U.S. forces assaulted dozens of suspected guerrilla positions, killing six alleged insurgents . . . amid a U.S. drive to intimidate the resistance. . . . Soldiers arrested an organizer of the fedayeen guerrillas."

Thugs, assassins, rebels, guerrillas, insurgents, resistance, fedayeen, not to mention *bad guys*—everybody has been struggling to find the right term for the enemy in Iraq. True, as long as it's unclear who is behind the attacks, it's probably prudent to cover all the bases. But the variation also signals a deeper problem in interpreting the story. The media may be making a valiant effort to cover the good news, but no one's sure what story line to wrap around the bad. Just which movie are we screening here?

Take "the resistance," which *Merriam-Webster's* defines as "an underground organization of a conquered or nearly conquered country engaging in sabotage and secret operations against occupation forces." That seems to fit the present situation on all counts, right down to the "or nearly conquered" part. But I can understand why papers like the *Los Angeles Times* would demur from describing the fighters as "the resistance." The name conjures up stirring World War II heroics à la *Casablanca* and *Passage to Marseille*, this before the French were recast as duplicitous surrender monkeys. You could see Sydney Greenstreet as Ahmad Chalabi, but Paul Bremer deserves better than Conrad Veidt.

The other words have problems too. The *American Heritage Dictionary* defines "insurgent" as "one that revolts against civil authority" and "rebellion" as "open, armed and organized resistance to a constituted government." But both words seem a little optimistic for Iraq right now, where civil authority and "constituted government" are thin on the ground. Then too, the words have awkward heroic resonances of their own: They bring to mind the good guys in *The Empire Strikes Back* or more disquietingly, *Lawrence of Arabia*. (I picture Alec Guinness saying, "The English have a great hunger for desolate places.")

Bush's "thugs" and "assassins" trail inauspicious associations of their own. The assassins were originally members of a radical Ismaili sect in medieval Syria who were sent out to murder the Crusaders by a reclusive ascetic known as "the old man of the mountains," who never was captured. (The name of the cult is derived from the hashish that its members were supposed to have chewed.) And thugs were originally the disciples of thuggee, the murderous Indian bandits that the British finally suppressed in the 1830s after a messy, decade-long campaign. The cult lives as a model for villains in Orientalist melodramas, from

Wilkie Collins' *The Moonstone* to *Indiana Jones and the Temple of Doom.*

For a while, Deputy Defense Secretary Paul Wolfowitz was pushing "bitter-enders," which brought to mind those Japanese holdouts in the caves of Saipan and Tarawa (recall Jeffrey Hunter in *Hell to Eternity*). But if you depict the task in Iraq as merely a mop-up operation, you have to acknowledge at some point that it isn't going very well.

Hence the shift to describing the situation as "a low-intensity conflict, a guerrilla war," as Bremer, the U.S. civilian administrator of the country, put it recently. Those terms put the engagements on a different footing—what were disturbing postwar security problems have now become merely minor skirmishes in an ongoing "postwar" (as a few journalists have taken to rendering the word) battle. When rockets were launched at two Baghdad hotels from donkey carts last week, Brig. Gen. Mark Kimmitt dismissed the attacks as a "militarily insignificant" effort to grab headlines. (And so they did—a Reuter's follow-up story was headed "Life worsens for Iraqi donkeys under U.S. suspicion," which sounded like a line from a plot summary of *The Secret of Santa Vittoria*.) But it was notable that Kimmitt went on to refer to the perpetrators with the singular "he" that soldiers have used since Kipling's day to confer a grudging respect on the enemy. "He's an inventive, ingenious enemy."

So it's understandable that some people should be looking for a new word for enemy that isn't charged with unwanted associations. Back in June, Bremer started to refer to those resisting the coalition presence as "rejectionists," adapting a term that has been used since the 1970s for Arab groups and governments opposed to a negotiated peace settlement with Israel. That use of the word has begun to pop up in other places—Sen. Joseph Biden (D-Del.) used it in a recent op-ed piece.

It would take quite a while for any new name to establish itself and for a story line to cohere around it, particularly if the screenplay has to be written from scratch. But it's looking as if there will be time for that.

[**Politics as Usual**]

So Sorry

The sociologist Erving Goffman used to talk about apologizing as a kind of "face-work," the maneuvers that help people get through their interactions with everybody's self-image intact. That sense of *face* comes from a translation of the Chinese expression for "lose face," *tio lien*. The phrase entered English in the 1860s, at a time when the Western powers were carving up China into zones of influence. The British had made some new demands, and when the Chinese resisted, the British sent a force headed by Lord Elgin to press their case. They burned the Summer Palace outside Beijing, but Elgin decided to spare the Forbidden City itself, fearing that its destruction would result in such a loss of face for the Manchus that the dynasty might fall—an unsettling prospect for Western trade. In the end, the British came out of the affair with some economic concessions, the Kowloon territory, and a useful new phrase. And while nowadays we talk about "losing face" in all sorts of contexts, the words still have a slightly orientalist ring.

So it wasn't surprising that journalists and politicians kept talking about the importance of saving face in connection with the incident last week when a U.S. spy plane was forced down in

Fresh Air Commentary, April 14, 2001

China. Some people argued that the Administration had to make some sort of verbal concession so that the Chinese could get out of the impasse in a face-saving way. But others claimed that any apology would cause the U.S. to lose face in Chinese eyes and weaken us in our further dealings with them. And when Bush's letter to the Chinese was released, those critics were quick to describe it using another expression borrowed from Chinese. As an editorial in *National Review* put it, "to apologize for a landing forced by Chinese recklessness . . . veers near kowtow territory."

Kowtow came into English after an earlier diplomatic confrontation between China and the West. In 1793, Great Britain sent Lord George Macartney to China as a trade envoy. The Chinese insisted that Macartney kowtow to the emperor, touching his forehead to the ground in a sign of submission. Macartney refused to do any more than bend his knee, as he would to an English sovereign. In his report he said that the Chinese had acceded to his conditions, though according to Chinese accounts he actually did touch his forehead. Probably Macartney's version was right—at least that would explain why he had to leave without the agreement he was after. But one way or the other, critics have been using the word ever since when anyone seems to be too deferential to China—people accused Bush's father of kowtowing when he refused to take a hard line towards the Chinese government after the Tiananmen massacres.

"Lose face," "kowtow"—when we borrow expressions like those, there's always the implication that we're in exotic cultural territory, and that these things matter more to the Chinese than they do to us. That perception was heightened last week when the Chinese versions of the American statement were released, and the newspapers called in language specialists to explain the subtleties of the translations. You came away with the impression that Chinese was a language with as many words for sorry as Eskimos are supposed to have for snow.

The American coverage made the whole affair sound like one of those familiar cross-cultural confrontations: a simple plain-spoken people with little patience for social rituals up against an Eastern culture that insists on elaborate shows of deference. But the fact is that when it comes to a belief in the ritual potency of apologies, Americans bow to no one. American public life has become a theater of contrition. Politicians ask forgiveness for their sexual and financial peccadilloes, athletes apologize for making racially insensitive remarks, journalists flagellate themselves when they're caught fabricating stories. And not a week goes by without some group calling for an official apology for some wrong that the government visited on them in the past.

In response, English has developed a vocabulary of penitence that can go verb-to-verb and adjective-to-adjective with any other language on earth. We have expressions for every gradation of responsibility and remorse. "Regrettable," "inexcusable," "an unfortunate error of judgment," "I acknowledge my personal responsibility," "We apologize for any inconvenience." The hard disks of corporate publicists are full of boilerplate mea culpas and nostra culpas to cover everything from oil spills to accounting irregularities. "Unacceptable" is a recent favorite here—"Our last quarter's revenues were unacceptable." It's an elegant way of appropriating the indignation without accepting the blame.

So when some suitably placating noises were called for last week, the State Department was up to the challenge. The only question is whether the Chinese were as adept at interpreting the U.S. response as Americans would be. After the U.S. statement was released, the Chinese media were announcing that the U.S. really had apologized for the collision. A lot of Americans were put out by that—there's nothing more irritating than to have somebody think you apologized when you know you damn well didn't.

Of course it's likely that those Chinese reports were just face-saving propaganda, like their claims about Lord Macartney's alleged kowtow to the emperor two hundred years ago. But you never know—maybe the Chinese really did miss some of the nuances of the American response. They may have a longer tradition of face-work than we do, but they've always gone about it in a very demonstrative way. They measure degrees of contrition by how deeply you prostrate your body; with us it can be simply a question of how sincerely you bite your lip.

Some of My Best Friends

In their serial cluelessness, Senator Trent Lott's apologies for his nostalgic remarks about Senator Strom Thurmond's segregationist presidential campaign in 1948 brought to mind a scene from Todd Haynes's *Far From Heaven*, which reimagines the domestic melodramas of the 1950s. At a Hartford art exhibition, the upper-middle-class housewife, Cathy Whitaker, runs into her black gardener. "I'm not prejudiced," she tells him. "Mr. Whitaker and I support equal rights for the Negro."

The line makes audiences titter. Whether or not we have put the mentalities of the 1950s behind us, the language of the period is as dated as pedal pushers and tailfins. It isn't just the reference to "the Negro," with that definite article that reduced a group to an exotic museum specimen (nobody ever talked about "the white" or "the Methodist"). Mrs. Whitaker's "I'm not prejudiced" is just as telling. It's hard to know which betrays its decade more, the word *prejudiced* or the character's ingenuous disavowal of it.

Prejudice wasn't a new word back then, of course, but it enjoyed a vogue in the '50s, particularly in the form of the bare adjective *prejudiced*, with no need to specify the object of dislike. The fashion owed a lot to the influential 1954 book *The Nature of*

Prejudice, by the Harvard psychologist Gordon Allport. Back then, in fact, *prejudice* had the flavor of other terms from social science that were flooding the language, like *juvenile delinquent, peer pressure,* and *status symbol.*

The postwar concern with prejudice signaled an acknowledgment of the pervasiveness of racial and religious antipathies. Before then, people tended to refer to those animosities with terms that didn't so much stigmatize the attitudes themselves as the vulgarity of taking them to excess. *Bigot,* for example, was a word of obscure origin that originally referred to a religious zealot, but which by the 1920s could be applied to someone with a narrow-minded animus against other races or religions. Still, it was a word that people associated more with Alabama sheriffs than with the demure country-club bias of the Connecticut suburbs.

In its way, the concern with prejudice signaled the optimism of a society that had just licked fascism and was looking hopefully toward the final triumph of tolerance. As Allport described it, prejudice was a superficial personality trait, rooted in the cognitive error of "faulty generalization." As such, prejudice was something you could learn to recognize in yourself and root out by assiduous mental housecleaning—a view that helped shape the faith in the remedial effects of integration.

Within a few years, though, that began to seem simplistic. *Prejudice* seemed to reduce all unwarranted animosities to a single pattern, whether they were directed against Jews, blacks, women, homosexuals, or the blind—or, for that matter, against Communists or Republicans. By the 1960s, those aversions all seemed to have had distinct etiologies and to merit different names, and over the coming decades *prejudice* was replaced by a whole lexicon of social pathologies: *anti-Semitism, xenophobia, racism, sexism, homophobia, ageism*—and still counting.

Apart from older terms like *anti-Semitism* and *xenophobia*, *racism* was the earliest and most potent of those terms. The word had actually been coined in the 1930s as a variant of *racialism*, to describe the racial doctrines of the fascists. By 1960, however, people were using the term to describe a personal or collective disposition that ran too deep to be accessible to cursory intro-spection. That was the Catch–22 of racism: If you denied it, you could be suspected of not really understanding what it was about. All of a sudden you could be held responsible for feelings you didn't know you had. "I'm not a racist" came to sound a bit like "I don't have any homosexual anxiety."

Racism and the other terms of the '60s blurred the distinction between thoughts and deeds. The social scientists of the 1950s had insisted that prejudice and discrimination were different things: Allport gave the example of an employer who dislikes Jews but treats them the same as anyone else. But *racism* sug-gested an unconscious attitude that invariably spilled over into behavior. And as if in sympathy, the word *bias* acquired the same ambiguity around this time, as people began to use it not just for a mental predilection but for the actions that followed from it, as in "housing bias."

Whatever the fortunes of the '60s social movements, their lin-guistic success was immediate and total. *Negro* was abandoned so rapidly that there were probably some Southerners who never used the word at all—they went straight from *colored* to *blacks*. And while *prejudice* has survived, its use in racial contexts has been declining. In a database of eighteen major newspapers, the relative frequency of phrases like "race prejudice" has declined by 60 percent since 1980, while the frequency of *racism* has doubled.

But those figures can be misleading. While the unrecon-structed right was quick to adopt the new language, in their mouths the words were less the marks of new concepts than the relabelings of old ones—not the discredited notions of the days of Jim Crow, but the notions that 1950s liberals had discarded when they left words like *prejudice* behind.

Listen to Senator Lott defending himself on the Black Entertainment Network (BET): "In order to be a racist, you have to feel superior. . . . I don't believe any man or any woman is superior to any other man or woman." That's pretty much the way someone like Allport would have defined *prejudice* in the '50s—as a simple matter of mistaken beliefs, and ones you can confidently reassure someone you don't harbor. Along with Lott's pointing to the blacks he had hired, his explanation suggested exactly the sort of comfortable assumptions people were rejecting when they abandoned *prejudice* for *racism* forty years ago—around the same time Americans were learning to smile at protestations of tolerance that began with "Some of my best friends . . ."

Consider the manner in which the right defends the vision of a "color-blind society," for example, in tones that echo the earnest speech the good-guy lieutenant or hospital administrator or baseball manager was always making in those "problem films" of the 1950s. As Sidney Poitier's medical supervisor put it in Joseph Mankiewicz's 1950 *No Way Out*: "I'm just pro good doctor—black, white, or polka-dot"—except that back then the point was to justify holding on to the doctor, not refusing to hire him. It's an odd code that the rear-guard right has been speaking in for the past forty years—using the words of the 1960s with the meanings of the '50s to convey the message of the '40s.

Interested Parties

Arnold Schwarzenegger may be a newcomer to California politics, but he has clearly been swatting up on the state's traditional rhetorical themes. He launched his campaign by pledging to become "the people's governor," vowing that he would accept no money from "the special interests who have a stranglehold on Sacramento." When it transpired that he had accepted contributions from developers and other wealthy individuals, he explained that those weren't special interests but merely "powerful interests who control things." What he had meant, he said, was only that he would refuse contributions from public employee unions or other groups he might have to negotiate with as governor. He apologized for the confusion about his fund-raising policy by saying, "I was not articulate enough to explain that."

In fairness to Schwarzenegger, he isn't the first politician to try to extricate himself from an apparent inconsistency by pleading linguistic ineptitude. And unlike others, he has the excuse of having come late to the English language and later still to the subtleties of its political patois. "Special interest" is a phrase that everyone uses selectively, after all. Schwarzenegger is merely guilty of having acknowledged explicitly what everyone else finds it prudent to leave unsaid.

The New York Times Week in Review, September 14, 2003

But the words that everyone takes for granted are usually the ones that work the most mischief in political life. The British politician Aneurin Bevan once noted that the student of politics "must always be on his guard against the old words, for the words persist when the reality behind them has changed."

As it happens, Schwarzenegger's campaign language, like the recall itself, is a legacy of the Progressive era. The recall process was adopted in 1911 under the governorship of the progressive reformer Hiram Johnson, who had been elected on the basis of a pledge much like Schwarzenegger's, to "return the government of California to the people." The difference was that in Johnson's case the "stranglehold" was exercised not by the public employee unions but by the Southern Pacific railroad—"the Octopus," as it was called, after the title of Frank Norris's 1880 novel about the struggle between the railroad and California wheat farmers. Like many progressives, Johnson put his faith in electoral reforms like the recall and the referendum, which "place in the hands of the people the means by which they may protect themselves."

The Progressive movement battened on that opposition between "the people" and "the interests," as people then referred to the trusts, corporations, and financial combines whose hold on American politics had been dramatically exposed in a series of scandals over the first decade of the century. Writing in 1922, in fact, Walter Lippmann noted that that rhetoric had become an electoral cliché. "The question of a proper fare on a municipal subway is symbolized as an issue between the People and the Interests...so that finally in the heat of a campaign, an eight cent fare becomes unAmerican. The Revolutionary fathers died to prevent it. Lincoln suffered that it might not come to pass, resistance to it was implied in the death of those who sleep in France."

Even so, the notion of "interest," in all its complexity, was central in the age's thinking about democracy. The word crops up over and over again in the writings of Henry Adams, Oliver Wendell Holmes, Herbert Croly, Lippmann, and John Dewey. It oscillates among personal, economic, and political meanings, as writers struggled to define the paramount political virtue of disinterestedness.

Much of the Progressives' language survived the era, along with their political reforms, but both were altered and denatured. By the time Robert LaFollette ran for president on the Progressive ticket in 1924, it was clear that "the interests" had adapted to the political and administrative reforms of the era. Money still talked, even if it had to speak a different dialect.

LaFollette was probably the last major politician to use the bald phrase "the interests." By the New Deal era, it had been replaced by "special interests," and later by the spin-off "special-interest groups." In those phrases, though, the meaning of "interest" was no longer restricted to economically powerful groups like corporations and, later, labor unions. By 1948, a letter-writer to *The New York Times* could describe opera fans as a special-interest group who shouldn't be subsidized by public funds. And in modern usage a special interest can be just about any group that favors a particular law or policy, invariably with the implication that its demands are at odds with the interests of "the people."

The *Weekly Standard* inveighs against "special interest legislation" like the California law that gives workplace protection for cross-dressing employees. An Enviromental Protection Agency administrator talks about the special interests who tried unsuccessfully to get greenhouse-gas emissions classified as pollutants. A sample grant application from the Minnesota Department of

Public Safety gives "anti-tobacco" as an example of a special interest group. And Hootie Johnson, the chairman of the Augusta National Golf Club, insists that the club will not "capitulate to special interest groups" by agreeing to admit women.

Those uses of "special interest" neatly obscure the difference between having an interest and being one. We may talk about banking interests or labor interests, but phrases like "the opera-lovers interest," "the women's interest," and "the cross-dressing interest" don't come easily to the tongue. The way "special interest" is used nowadays, it blurs the distinction between the economic and political senses of *interest* that the Progressives struggled to reconcile. Now everyone is "interested," in the old sense of the word—the environmentalists as much as the car-makers, the American Cancer Society as much as the tobacco companies.

The passing of the Progressives' notion of interest took disinterestedness over the side along with it. It was just about the time that the meaning of *interest* was becoming blurred that American language critics began to lament the tendency to use *disinterested* to mean "uninterested." In fact, that usage had been around for centuries, but it suddenly seemed a harbinger of the disappearance of the old, "noble" use of the word to mean, roughly, "impartial." As it happens, the "impartial" sense still accounts for the majority of uses of *disinterested* in the press. But it isn't a word that comes up much when we try to define political virtue. There's no position that's free from what William Dean Howells called "the sordid competition of interests," now that *interest* itself has been given so broad a charter.

Yet there's one feature of the progressives' notion of interest that has survived. We still think of special interests as groups that have obtained a back-door influence on law or policy, whether it's purchased by campaign contributions or bartered for political support. Whether the word is applied to women's groups or tobacco companies, the implication is that they wouldn't be able to put their views across in a direct popular appeal.

What's notable is how many influences that definition exempts—corporations that take out advertisements or create foundations to promote their political opinions, people who buy newspapers or television networks to disseminate their views, millionaires who use their own money to finance their political ambitions or a recall election. Those aren't special interests, but merely "powerful interests who control things," as Schwarzenegger put it. Hiram Johnson would have found nothing to fault in that language, either.

Me Too, Too

"No more me-tooism," wrote John Hood in *National Review* recently, as President Bush was announcing his prescription drug program. That's the familiar charge when politicians from either side seem to be sacrificing ideological commitment to expediency. "I'm getting to the point where I think it's better to lose with someone like [Howard Dean]," one Democrat was quoted as saying, "than to have all this me-tooism."

"Me too" began its life as a verb. Just after the 1940 election, Harold Ickes, Franklin Roosevelt's adviser, wrote in his diary that the Republican candidate Wendell Willkie had "overlooked the best chance that he had by being content merely to 'me too' the president . . . instead of striking out for himself in a bold and positive way."

The noun *me-tooism* followed in 1949. The postwar period was fond of using *-ism* to coin jaunty names for new trends and doctrines, with items like *me-firstism*, *eggheadism*, *against-ism*, *mom-ism*, *big-shotism*, *nice-nellieism*, and *go-it-aloneism*. It was a way of mocking the more portentously philosophical isms that were in vogue in the first half of the century, the fashion that Westbrook Pegler ridiculed in 1951 as "galloping ismatism."

The New York Times Week in Review, July 13, 2003

But despite its form, *me-tooism* was really the ismatist's reproach to the apostasies of Republican centrists. Campaigning against Dwight D. Eisenhower in the 1952 primaries, Senator Robert A. Taft warned that a "me too" strategy would alienate the Republican Party's conservative base while making few inroads in the mugwump vote—a voter he defined as "an intellectual sitting on a fence with his mug on one side and his wump on another."

Eisenhower's me-tooism was both substantive and symbolic. It isn't easy to say which of the isms he espoused was more exasperating to conservatives—the welfare statism of the New Deal programs he supported, or the middle-of-the-roadism that he took for a motto, endorsing conservatism in economic matters and liberalism in "human affairs."

That strategy effectively undercut the liberal rhetoric of his Democratic opponent, Adlai Stevenson, in the 1952 and 1956 presidential elections, but over the coming decades the Republicans remained a minority party, rent by charges of me-tooism and extremism. Eisenhower never forgave Barry Goldwater for describing his administration as a "dime-store New Deal." But Goldwater's resolutely un-me-too campaign of 1964 got nowhere with its slogan, "A choice, not an echo," and it wasn't until Ronald Reagan's victory in 1980 that the Republicans successfully reinvented themselves in what Ickes would have called a "bold and positive" way.

Charges of me-tooism didn't surface again until the 1990s, when another popular president faced with a large opposition majority adopted a strategy of "triangulation" between the left and right. President Clinton's middle-of-the-roadism riled not just his party's own left, but conservatives who saw it as a sign of devious pusillanimity. "Clinton has become the first prominent 'me-too' Democrat," the conservative columnist Tony Snow wrote in 1994, "someone who accepts the fundamental rightness of his opponents' cause but doesn't have the stomach to go where the principles lead."

But when it became clear that the confrontational rhetoric of Newt Gingrich's "Contract with America" was alienating many voters, Republicans found themselves having to do some me-too-ing of their own. The new look made its debut at the party's 1996 convention, and was in full display in George W. Bush's 2000 campaign. Democrats had their turn to become indignant when Bush's nomination acceptance speech appropriated some of Clinton's own phraseology, like "Medicare reflects our values as a society."

Since then Bush and the Republicans have proved adroit at neutralizing the Democrats' traditional rhetorical advantages on issues like education and the environment. Thanks to the word-smith Frank Luntz, the Republicans have stopped talking about rolling back regulations in favor of appeals to "balanced, common-sense solutions."

And "inclusiveness" has never been so inclusive. At one time or another the White House has applied the word to Republican efforts to increase recruiting among women and minorities, the Homeland Security Department, Vice President Dick Cheney's energy task force, the Coalition of the Willing, post-Hussein Iraq, and Senator Rick Santorum of Pennsylvania (an "inclusive man," Bush called him, after his remarks equating homosexuality with incest and bigamy).

Bush is hardly an Eisenhower Republican, of course. He's not about to style himself a "progressive moderate," much less warn against the dangers of the military-industrial complex. But even if his me-tooism is largely symbolic—and highly selective, at that—it has left the Democrats in a rhetorical bind. Unlike the 1950s, this is a period of sharp partisan divisions over most important issues, and yet the Democrats are struggling to find language that makes their differences with the Administration clear. The phrases that signaled many of the great themes of liberalism—"inclusiveness," "community," "corporate responsibility"—have become bland, universally sanctioned values that no longer connote the political program that brought them to the ball.

Granted, this is partly due to a propensity for overcomplexity that has always plagued the Democrats—as Joe Klein has observed, lousy bumper stickers are a chronic Democratic woe. But the Democrats are also the victims of a shift in the linguistic center of gravity. Now, as in the past, frequent complaints of me-tooism are a sign that the language of the last generation of isms is losing its hold on the political imagination.

For the first time in history, in fact, the 'me-too' label is as likely to be applied to one side as to the other. That doesn't signal a rush to the center, but it does mark the waning of another cycle of isms, as people weary of grand doctrines that offer themselves as the motor forces of history, and history takes one of its ideological breathers.

It's inevitable that *conservatism* will suffer the same decline as *liberalism*—an oppositional label can't flourish for long when its contrary is ailing. (Nowadays, it's the right that is most responsible for keeping the liberal label alive.) President Bush's use of "compassionate conservatism" was an implicit acknowledgment of the uneasiness that many voters have about the unqualified noun. And Luntz's advice to Republicans to refrain from describing opponents as liberals suggests his awareness of the public's increasing impatience with purely ideological wrangling.

In fact, the forces that severed liberal rhetoric from its underlying ideology cut both ways. As Democrats have begun to realize, traditional conservative themes like fiscal discipline, wealth creation, and individual freedom are up for grabs. Both sides will be trying to stake out a new political vocabulary, as they contest the meanings of words like *security, opportunity, responsibility,* and *fairness.* Those may seem like vague terms, but then so did *conservatism* and *liberalism* when the modern opposition between the two was taking shape in the early years of Roosevelt's presidency. As late as 1936, Herbert Hoover was accusing Roosevelt of a kind of me-tooism avant la lettre for hijacking the true meaning of *liberal.*

Charges of me-tooism are inevitable in periods of terminological realignment. New political vocabularies always sound nebulous until debate gives them partisan shape and color. But as no one knows better than we San Franciscans, the distinctive features of the landscape sooner or later emerge out of the fog.

Slippery Slopes

I read in recent months that Democrats were complaining that the Administration's prescription-drug bill would put the nation on the slippery slope toward Medicare privatization, that the dismantling of West Bank outposts puts Israel on a slippery slope leading to its destruction, and that the ownership of a women's NBA team by a Connecticut casino sets the sport on a slippery slope towards control by gamblers.

And the metaphor was predictably ubiquitous in condemnations of the Supreme Court's overturning of the Texas sodomy law—Jerry Falwell said the ruling could set the nation down a slippery slope in which courts might approve bestiality, prostitution, and the use of narcotics, in an echo of a controversial remark by Senator Rick Santorum several weeks previously.

To judge from the news stories, the entire nation is coming to resemble San Francisco after a heavy rainfall. In the press, the phrase "slippery slope" is more than seven times as common as it was twenty years ago. It's a convenient way of warning of the dire effects of some course of action without actually having to criticize the action itself, which is what makes it a favorite ploy of hypocrites: "Not that there's anything wrong with A, mind you, but A will lead to B and then C, and before you know it we'll be up to our armpits in Z."

The argument goes by various names. The phrase "slippery slope" dates from the mid-nineteenth century, around the same time that people started to talk about "letting the camel's nose into the tent." That's an allusion to a fable about a camel who asks if he can put his nose into a workman's tent to keep it from the cold, and winds up inserting first his shoulders, then his legs, and so on, until he disposseses the inhabitant. Actually, I haven't been able to find any Arab source for the fable, and it may very well be a Victorian invention. There's a version of the tale in an 1860 poem by Lydia Howard Sigourney, which concludes:

> Oh, youthful hearts, to gladness born,
> Treat not this Arab lore with scorn.
> To evil habit's earliest wile
> Lend neither ear, nor glance, nor smile,
> Choke the dark fountain ere it flows,
> Nor even admit the Camel's Nose.

Then there's the domino effect, an analogy that Dwight Eisenhower used in 1954 to justify U.S. intervention in Vietnam. Or people talk about *the thin end of the wedge, the snowball effect, the doomsday scenario,* or *opening the floodgates.* Philosophers have sometimes tried to distinguish the various arguments on logical grounds, but usage always blurs the lines between them—one way or another, it always comes down to "God knows where will it all end."

The rhetoric textbooks usually describe the "slippery slope" as a logical fallacy, but that depends on how it's used. When you say that A puts us on a slippery slope to B, you might mean only that A will create political momentum for B, or that A would make B cheaper or easier to implement. The UCLA law professor Eugene Volokh gives the example of installing video cameras at every intersection. That may make it easier to deter street crime, but it also provides the government with the means to perform more sinister forms of surveillance.

Or sometimes the slippery slope is invoked in the course of making an argument about the impossibility of drawing clear moral distinctions—if you can't draw the line between A and B, then how can you accept one and reject the other? That's an argument you often hear from abortion critics—where does a fetus end and a child begin? It's an instance of what Greek philosophers called the fallacy of the heap, or the Sorites Fallacy. If you start with a heap of sand and take one grain away, you're still left with a heap, but if you keep repeating the process you wind up saying that a single grain of sand is a heap all by itself. The mistake is in assuming that if a distinction isn't clear-cut it can't be drawn at all—a form of argument you could use to discredit the distinctions between *young* and *old*, *slow* and *fast*, or *bitter* and *sweet*, if you were of a mind to, until all of experience was reduced to a featureless muddle.

The Supreme Court justices love to torment advocates with slippery slope examples to get them to clarify their positions, with the result that the Court transcripts often have the air of absurdist theater. But the technique is more disconcerting when it moves from the hypothetical to assertions of fact, the way it did in Justice Antonin Scalia's dissent in the case overturning the Texas sodomy statute. According to Scalia, once you start throwing out laws that reflect the moral choices of the majority, you undermine the basis for state laws against bigamy, same-sex marriage, adult incest, prostitution, masturbation, adultery, fornication, bestiality, and obscenity. (That reads as if Scalia intended to warn supporters of anti-masturbation statutes that the Texas sodomy decision puts these laws on shaky grounds. And so it does, provided, of course, that the act is consensual.)

I have the feeling that Scalia had a good time drawing up that list, but it isn't likely he really buys the logic. It's hard to imagine him voting to overturn a state anti-bestiality statute on the grounds that the Texas sodomy decision leaves him no alternative.

But the real problem with slippery-slope arguments isn't their logic, but the rhetorical games people play with them—they're a way of turning every decision into an unprecedented step into the void. In theory, you could use Scalia's logic to run the metaphor uphill; you could just as easily say that refusing to overturn the Texas statute would open the way to laws restricting nose rings, public dancing, or other things that voters might find morally unacceptable. But people rarely mention the slippery slope to argue for a change in law or policy—it's chiefly an argument for maintaining the status quo. The English legal scholar Glanville Williams once called the slippery slope "the trump card of the traditionalist, because no proposal for reform is immune to [it]."

That comes from the metaphor itself, with its image of stepping off the edge of a slope. But law and policy decisions are rarely that dramatic—it's more like carving our way along a hillside, making small adjustments as we go. Or to switch metaphors, we all agree that we want to keep the camel's nose inside the tent and leave his nether parts out in the desert—the question always comes down to where we want to put the hump.

If It's Orwellian, It's Probably Not

On George Orwell's centenary—he was born on June 25, 1903—the most telling sign of his influence is the words he left us with: not just *thought police, doublethink,* and *unperson,* but also *Orwellian* itself, the most widely used adjective derived from the name of a modern writer. In the press and on the Internet, it's more common than *Kafkaesque, Hemingwayesque,* and *Dickensian* put together. It even noses out the rival political reproach *Machiavellian,* which had a 500-year head start.

Eponyms are always the narrowest sort of tribute, though. *Orwellian* doesn't have anything to do with Orwell as a socialist thinker, or for that matter, as a human being. People are always talking about Orwell's decency, but "Orwellian decency" would be an odd phrase indeed. And *Orwellian* commemorates Orwell the writer only for three of his best known works: the novels *Animal Farm* and *1984* and the essay "Politics and the English Language." The adjective reduces Orwell's palette to a single shade of noir. It brings to mind only sordid regimes of surveillance and thought control and the distortions of language that make them possible.

Orwell's views on language will probably outlive his political

ideas. At least they seem to require no updating or apology,
whereas his partisans feel the need to justify the continuing rele-
vance of his politics. Yet Orwell was scarcely the first writer to
protest against political euphemism. More than 150 years earlier,
Edmund Burke sounded a very Orwellian note in his attacks on
the apologists for the French Revolution who tried to extenuate
the September Massacres of 1792: "The whole compass of the
language is tried to find sinonimies and circumlocutions for massacre and murder. Things are never called by their common
names. Massacre is sometimes *agitation*, sometimes *effervescence*,
sometimes *excess*; sometimes too continued an exercise of *a revolutionary power*."

But it was Orwell who popularized the modern picture of
language as the active accomplice of power, whether by conceal-
ing its abuses or, as with Newspeak, by making dissent literally
unthinkable. In "Politics and the English Language," he wrote
that "Political language . . . is designed to make lies sound truthful
and murder respectable," and spoke of "words that fall upon the
facts like soft snow, blurring the outlines and covering up all the
details."

That was an appealing notion to an age that had learned to be
suspicious of ideologies, and critics on all sides have found it useful to cite "Politics and the English Language" in condemning the
equivocations of their opponents. Critics on the left hear
Orwellian resonances in phrases like "weapons of mass protection," or in names like the Patriot Act or the Homeland Security
Department's Operation Liberty Shield, which authorizes indefinite detention of asylum-seekers from certain nations. Critics on
the right hear them in phrases like "reproductive health services,"
"Office of Equality Assurance," and "English Plus," for bilingual

education. And just about everyone discerned an Orwellian note in the name of the Pentagon's Total Information Awareness project, which was aimed at mining a vast centralized database of personal information for patterns that might reveal terrorist activities. (The name was finally changed to the Terrorist Information Awareness program, in an effort to reassure Americans who have nothing to hide.)

Of course, where one side sees deceptive packaging, the other is likely to see only effective branding. But there's something troubling in the easy use of the label *Orwellian*, as if these phrases committed the same sorts of linguistic abuses that led to the gulags and the death camps. In fact the specters that *Orwellian* conjures aren't really the ones we have to worry about. Newspeak may have been a plausible invention in 1948, when totalitarian thought control still seemed an imminent possibility. But the collapse of Communism revealed the bankruptcy not just of the Stalinist social experiment, but of its linguistic experiments as well. After seventy-five years of incessant propaganda, "socialist man" turned out to be a cynic who didn't even believe the train schedules.

Political language is still something to be wary of, but it doesn't work as Orwell feared. In fact the modern language of control is more effective than Soviet Newspeak precisely because it's less bleak and intimidating. Think of the way business has been re-engineering the language of ordinary interaction in the interest of creating "high-performance corporate cultures." To a reanimated Winston Smith, there would be something wholly familiar in being told that he had to file an annual "vision statement" or that he should henceforth eliminate "problems" from his vocabulary in favor of "issues." But the hero of *1984* would find the whole exercise much more convivial than the Two-Minute Hate at the Ministry of Truth. And he'd be astonished to see management condoning its employees' playing buzzword bingo and posting Dilbert strips on the walls of their cubicles.

For Orwell, the success of political jargon and euphemism required an uncritical or even unthinking audience: A "reduced state of consciousness," as he put it, was "favorable to political conformity." As things turned out, though, the political manipulation of language seems to thrive on the critical skepticism that Orwell encouraged. In fact, there has never been an age that was so well-schooled in the perils of deceptive language or in decoding political and commercial messages, as witness the official canonization of Orwell himself. Thanks to the schools, *1984* is probably the best-selling political novel of modern times (current Amazon sales rank: No. 93), and "Politics and the English Language" is the most widely read essay about the English language—and very likely in it as well.

But as advertisers have known for a long time, no audience is easier to beguile than one that is smugly confident of its own sophistication. The word *Orwellian* contributes to that impression. Like *propaganda*, it implies an aesthetic judgment more than a moral one. Calling an expression Orwellian means not that it's deceptive but that it's crudely deceptive.

Today, the real damage isn't done by the euphemisms and circumlocutions that we're likely to describe as Orwellian. *Ethnic cleansing, revenue enhancement, voluntary regulation, tree-density reduction, faith-based initiatives, extra affirmative action*—those terms may be oblique, but at least they wear their obliquity on their sleeves.

Rather, the words that do the most political work are simple ones—*jobs and growth, family values,* and *color-blind,* not to mention *life* and *choice.* Concrete words like these are the hardest ones to see through—they're opaque when you hold them up to the light. Orwell knew that, of course. "To see what is in front of one's nose needs a constant struggle." It's not what you'd call an Orwellian sentiment, but it's very like the man.

Meetings of the Minds

Like all difficult negotiations, the Mideast talks that began last week will require some careful delicate footwork—a point that became clear when Israeli Prime Minister Ariel Sharon took the step of referring to the Israeli "occupation," and then issued a statement "clarifying" the remark the following day.

In that context, no word is more charged than *compromise*, a notion that's easier to disavow than embrace. "There can be no compromise with terror," Sharon said in his English-language speech at the Middle East summit in Jordan, and Palestinian Prime Minister Mahmoud Abbas vowed to fight terrorism in words that were translated as "without compromise." But neither leader seemed inclined to talk about compromise in a positive way. If the Israelis and Palestinians are willing to make compromises in the interest of a settlement, they're not about to put it that way just now.

According to some people, in fact, Arabs find compromise literally unspeakable. That was the conclusion of an article that appeared in the Egyptian newspaper *Al-Ahram* in September 2002. Its author was an Egyptian businessman and writer named Tarek Heggy, who claimed the Arabs have never developed a "culture of compromise"—in fact, he said, Arabic doesn't even have a word for that notion. For the Arabs, he said, compromise is associated with submission, retreat, and weakness, whereas the Anglo-Saxon nations value the ideas of compromise and a respect for the opinions of others. Heggy's article was widely circulated on the Web, and several writers were quick to attach a political significance to the absence of an Arabic word for compromise—as one put it, "No wonder there are problems negotiating peace."

Heggy's claim has a familiar ring. You're always hearing people say, "The so-and-so people don't have a word for such-and-such," where the absence of the word is supposed to shed a telling light on a people's culture. At one time or another, I've heard it said that French doesn't have a word for "nice," that German doesn't have a word for "fair play," and that Chinese doesn't have a word for "privacy." Back in 1985, President Reagan asserted that the Russian language didn't have a word for freedom. (Of course it does—*svoboda*—but Reagan was never one to let details get in the way of a good story.)

Of course it often happens that another language won't have any easy way of referring to something that's important to English speakers (and vice-versa, *ça va sans dire*). But that's usually because the concept itself is one its speakers can live without. You're not surprised to learn that Tibetan doesn't have words for "squeeze play" or "happy hour." But it's hard to imagine how any people could conduct the commerce and politics of a major civilization without having a way of talking about compromise. What's going on in all those souks—is everybody paying retail? And how would a people with no concept of compromise manage their domestic life? "She wanted to spend all our holidays with her family, and I wanted to spend them all with mine. So we divorced."

In fact, when I asked a couple of Arabic linguists about this, they confirmed for me that Arabic has several expressions that translate the English *compromise*, though none is a single word. (The phrase that Abbas's translator rendered as "without compromise" actually contained a classical Arabic word that came closer to "relenting," but then the English *uncompromising* really means something like "unrelenting," too.)

When speakers of colloquial Arabic want to talk about compromise, they use phrases like "we reached a middle ground." But then English often expresses this notion with a phrase, too—we talk about reaching a meeting of the minds, striking a balance, finding a happy medium, or meeting someone halfway. Before Shakespeare's time, in fact, English lacked a single verb for compromise, and was none the worse for it.

The fact is that people have many more concepts than can be expressed in a single word in their languages. Take the German *Schadenfreude*, which denotes the pleasure we take in the misfortunes of others. It's a nice item to have handy in a pre-packaged form. But Red Sox fans don't have to learn German before they can enjoy watching the Yankees drop eight straight at home. And even if their language lacks a single word for "cozy," Germans aren't insensible to the pleasures of an armchair by a warm fire on a winter's night.

So why do people find these factoids about missing words so alluring? One reason, no doubt, is that they can serve to garb old-fashioned ethnic stereotypes in respectable linguistic attire. Westerners have always attributed an unwillingness to compromise to the Arabs and the other Semitic peoples. T. E. Lawrence claimed that the Semites "had no half-tones in their register of vision," and described them as "a people of primary colours, or rather of black and white, who saw the world always in contour." And the English historian Elizabeth Monroe explained the failure of the British government's 1937 partition plan for Palestine by saying that the British were "full of capacity for compromise" and couldn't understand that they were dealing with "two peoples belonging to the most uncompromising race in the world." The only difference is that back then, nobody felt the need to lay the obstinacy of the Jews or the Arabs to their lack of a word for compromise—people just assumed that obstinacy was bred in the Semitic bone.

But every people has conflicting views of compromise, however they express the notion. The vaunted flexibility of the Anglo-Saxon peoples wasn't much in evidence in the months before the Iraq war, when the United States was adamantly refusing to strike a deal that would allow the United Nations inspectors more time to seek out Iraq's weapons of mass destruction. At the time, the Administration was describing the Security Council's position as "appeasement," the word we English speakers use when we want to equate compromise with submission and weakness.

One could even argue that the English language betrays a strain of ethnic stubbornness, as well. Take the way we use *uncompromising* as a morally complimentary term nowadays. "She's an uncompromising perfectionist"—why is that necessarily a good thing? And why is it that the adjective *compromised* can only have a negative meaning—"The ambassador was too compromised to serve as an intermediary"?

All that that shows is that languages provide their speakers with many ways to talk about compromise, depending on whether they're in the mood to strike a deal. Someone who is seen as uncompromising on Monday can come to seem inflexible or stubborn by the end of the week, when the negotiations come down to the wire. If the players really want to reach a compromise in the Middle East, they'll find the words for it.

Lattes, Limousines, and Libs

The announcement that two Chicago venture capitalists will finance a liberal talk radio network met with the skepticism that might greet the formation of a pro badminton circuit. Some conservatives said that liberal dogma couldn't withstand the rough and tumble of talk radio (which is "ultimately about ideas," as Thomas Sowell put it), the implication being that the left has no thinkers with the gravitas of a Limbaugh or a Liddy. Others said that liberals just can't be funny—the left has no wits like Limbaugh and Liddy, either—while the blogger Antic Muse said there are funny liberals, but they're working in Hollywood. Still others said liberals won't engage in demagogy, that liberals are afraid of offending their constituencies, that liberals are boring policy wonks, or that liberals are too nuanced for the AM drive-time crowd.

Well, but hold it right there. If we're really looking to understand the success of right-wing talk radio, we needn't go much further than people's readiness to start sentences with "Liberals are..." and to go on to describe liberalism as something between a personality disorder and a market segment.

That's what the radio hosts batten on. They understand that

The New York Times Week in Review, March 2, 2003

their listeners respond more immediately to attacks on the phonies up the block than on more remote objects of indignation. Not that the hosts and callers don't have a deep antipathy to Saddam Hussein, criminals, illegal immigrants, and the United Nations, but those miscreants tend to serve only as the pretext for denunciations of the people who coddle them—the libs, as Limbaugh calls them. The familiar tone of that epithet has more to do with creating an "us" than a "them"; it distinguishes the show's audience from the political dimwits who haven't cottoned to the menace in their midst.

Talk radio didn't invent the negative branding of liberals. It began to emerge about twenty-five years ago, around the time when words like *lifestyle* and *yuppie* first entered the general vocabulary, as marketers replaced sociologists as the cartographers of the American social landscape. Phrases like "Volvo liberal" and "the Chablis-and-brie set" were already well established when the liberal Republican John Anderson made his presidential bid in 1980.

Those labels are different from older descriptions like "limousine liberal," which evoke the image of liberals as wealthy hypocrites. The new vocabulary makes consumer preferences the most telling signs of personal values, so that it seems natural for Richard Lowry, editor of *National Review*, to talk about the "'tall skim double-mocha latte, please' culture of contemporary America."

Some conservatives have tried to take that connection seriously. David Brooks has tied urban liberals' fondness for expensive coffee drinks to their predilection for inconspicuous consumption. They avoid the traditional luxuries of "vulgar Republicans," preferring to spend extravagantly on items that used to be cheap, like coffee, bread, and water, or on products that seem to answer to practical needs, like Volvos or hiking boots. Yet you can find a Starbucks outlet and a Volvo dealership in Franklin County, Pennsylvania, the locale where Brooks has done his weekend ethnography of pro-Bush America, not to mention other red-state bastions like Lubbock, Texas, Cheyenne, Wyoming, and Murfreesboro, Tennessee. However those retailers choose their locations, it isn't by looking for concentrations of liberal guilt.

Phrases like "latte liberal" and "Volvo liberals" have nothing to do with what anybody actually buys—they're pure plays on brand aura. Liberals are the sort of people you would expect to drink an expensive, milky coffee concoction and to drive a safe, practical car from socialist Sweden, whatever the actual facts of the marketplace are. (Actually, an article in *American Demographics* reports that the great majority of brie consumers are moderate Republicans—not surprising, considering that brie is an upscale product. In the luxury marketplace, demographics always trumps ideology.)

The success of that branding strategy extends well beyond opinion columns and talk radio. In major newspapers, the phrases "middle-class liberals" and "middle-class Democrats" are used with about the same frequency. But "working-class liberals" is almost nonexistent; it's outnumbered by "working-class Democrats" by about 30 to 1. It's as if you can't count as a liberal until you can afford to indulge yourself.

By contrast, the press talks about "working-class conservatives" and "working-class Republicans" with about the same frequency. In fact there are many more mentions of working-class conservatives than of working-class liberals, which creates a strange picture of American political attitudes.

You see the same discrepancies when you substitute terms like "black," "Hispanic," or "minority" in those patterns. As the media tell the story, minorities and members of the working class can qualify only as Democrats; liberalism is a mind-set restricted to the white middle class.

But branding is a game that two could play, if liberals cared to leaven substance with style themselves. In their efforts to bond with the working class, conservative pundits can be as risibly phony and pretentious as anything that Hollywood or the Upper West Side has to offer. You think of Bill O'Reilly describing himself as a "working-class guy"—this from an accountant's son who grew up in Waterbury, Long Island. Or listen to Ann Coulter, who grew up in New Canaan, Connecticut, and her paean to New York's other boroughs, as reported in *The New York Times*: "Queens, baseball games—those are my people. American people."

Then there's Lowry, a University of Virginia grad, who admits to having no familiarity with motorcycles but nonetheless holds that he would rather be governed by 2,000 motorcyclists than all the Volvo drivers in the United States.

That's a plight that the privileged pundits of the right can't escape: Their politics turns them into traitors to their demographic. You have to feel a certain sympathy for all those Yale and Dartmouth grads at *National Review* and *The American Spectator* who feel obliged to eschew Chardonnay and latte in favor of Budweiser and Maxwell House. One way or the other, modern politics makes fashion victims of us all.

Where the Left Commences

The left-right spectrum was born in revolutionary France, but Americans didn't adopt it until the New Deal era. It seems to lay out the political topography in a conveniently symmetrical way, to the point where some have felt that you could determine the "balance" of the media simply by counting how often each of the labels appears.

But the linguistic landscape is a lot more corrugated and uneven than it appears. Take *leftist*. As a pair with *rightist*, it had a long history as a purely descriptive term before the McCarthyites adopted it as a label for Communist sympathizers and subversive organizations. Just before the 1952 election, Senator Joseph R. McCarthy accused Adlai Stevenson of being unfit for the presidency because of his association with "leftists" like Arthur M. Schlesinger Jr., who had defended the right of Communists to teach in universities (provided, Schlesinger added, that "they do not disqualify themselves by intellectual distortions in the classroom"). And in the same year, Americans for Democratic Action indignantly denied charges that it was a leftist group, pointing out that it had worked at "purging the American liberal movement of individuals with loyalties to Communism."

The New York Times Week in Review, August 17, 2003

Leftist was not a word to be used lightly, even by the right. In a 1954 editorial, the *Wall Street Journal* worried that McCarthy's "slam-bang denunciations of . . . 'leftist' influence" were making him a "depreciating asset" to the Republican Party, with the quotation marks around "leftist" holding the word at arm's length.

By all linguistic rights, the leftist label should have disappeared from the lexicon as McCarthyism faded, and as labels like *communistic, fellow traveler,* and *Communist sympathizer* (or *comsymp* for short) were going the way of the poodle skirt. But *leftist* lingered, shifting its reference to antiwar demonstrators. Only after the Vietnam War did the word begin to decline as an epithet, though it was still routinely used in foreign news reports.

Then, in the late 1990s, *leftist* underwent a sudden revival. The word is 50 percent more frequent in major newspapers and magazines now than it was five years ago, with almost all the increase a result of its use as a label for domestic groups and individuals. Apart from the odd reference to Angela Davis or the Spartacist League, *leftist* nowadays is almost never used for old-style radicals or Marxists. In fact it was the eclipse of the movement left and the fall of Communism that freed the word to serve as a phantom finger that the right could wave in the culture wars.

In 1954, the Girl Scouts of America was labeled a leftist organization when the American Legion and the House Committee on Un-American Activities accused it of permitting an ex-Communist to serve as a troop leader and of using a handbook that preached "U.N. and World Government propaganda." When the leftist charge is repeated now, it's because the scouts permit lesbians to be troop leaders and support programs like Title IX.

A few years ago, a contributor to *National Review* urged Republicans to purge "leftist influences" from the party, citing the support of Governor Jane Swift of Massachusetts for legal abortion. An opinion piece in the *Morning Call* of Allentown, Pennsylvania, called Senator Arlen Specter a leftist for his support of cloning research and gay rights, and other commentators have applied the word to senators like Lincoln Chafee, Byron L. Dorgan, and James M. Jeffords, not to mention liberal evergreens like Senators Charles E. Schumer and Edward M. Kennedy. On the Web, Martin Sheen and Susan Sarandon are more likely to be labeled leftists than Fidel Castro is. And Jerry Falwell's *National Liberty Journal* has attached the word to the Dixie Chicks—an odd choice to inherit the mantle of Pete Seeger and Woody Guthrie.

It's getting hard to tell leftists and liberals apart without an agenda. Hence the increasing popularity of *liberal-leftist*, which merges categories on the model of compounds like *toaster-oven* and *owner-occupier*. (Linguists call those compounds "dvandvas," a term invented by the Sanskrit grammarians.) Peggy Noonan has used the double-l word to describe abortion-rights groups, and during Hillary Rodham Clinton's Senate race, the conservative commentator John Podhoretz described her as "running as an unapologetic liberal-leftist."

But liberal Democrats never describe themselves as leftists, not even apologetically. (For that matter, there aren't many who are willing to describe themselves as liberals, either.) That's the fundamental asymmetry of the left-right distinction in American politics. Historically, the left commences where liberalism ends. But conservatives have never demurred from placing themselves on the right, letting qualifiers like *mainstream* and *extremist* do the work of sorting out the bow-tied Alsopians from the fatigues-wearing abolish-the-I.R.S. crowd. True, many conservatives are uneasy about the label *right wing*, and though a few call themselves rightists, the word sounds too exotic for most to put it on their business cards. But no one feels the need for a compound like *conservative-rightist*—there's no distinction to blur in the first place.

The new uses of *leftist* exploit that asymmetry. They're aimed at nudging the political center to the right, by portraying social liberals as radicals outside the mainstream. That's a risky semantic maneuver. In any tug of war between a label and the things it's attached to, the label ultimately loses. Sometimes it's simply diluted to the point of meaninglessness. That happened with the fascist label after the American left began to throw it around indiscriminately in the 1970s, and it may very well be the fate of *imperialist* now. But the leftist label is less likely to be superannuated than drawn back into the center. Describing the Girl Scouts or Arlen Specter as leftist doesn't demonize them so much as make the epithet itself sound less alarming.

You can already sense a weakening in the meaning of leftist in the way some conservatives use the "liberal-leftist" combination, treating *liberal* as a modifying adjective. The Republican minority leader of the South Carolina Senate described a Democratic legislator as "one of the most liberal leftists that we have in the House," and a letter-writer to the *Palm Beach Post* decried the influence of "extremely liberal leftists" in academia. Fifty years ago, those phrases would have sounded dyslexic—don't you mean "extremely leftist liberals"? Now they suggest that *liberal* outflanks *leftist* in many people's minds.

Some will be unhappy about seeing *leftist* become a mainstream category, not least people who still wear the label defiantly. But there's this to say for it: The center divider would line up with the middle of the road.

A Fascist in Every Garage

When I lived in Rome many years ago, one of the best late-night gelato bars was a place in the upscale Parioli district that was frequented by the *jeunesse dorée* of the neighborhood, most of whom were partisans of the neo-fascist Italian Social Movement. "Passiamo per i fascisti strada facendo," people would say when they came out of a movie—"Let's stop by the fascists on the way home."

You wouldn't hear that sort of familiar reference from Americans. Fascism has never really figured as an indigenous category of our political life, the way it has in Italy and other European nations. Not that we haven't had our own right-wing fringe groups, but we usually call them by other names, like kooks or extremists, and we don't generally expect to run into them dressed in Armani when we go to the ice-cream parlor. But that point might not be immediately obvious just by looking at newspapers or the Web, particularly now that *fascist* is back in fashion. It's a word we throw around as easily as *bastard*, and with no more heed to its literal meaning.

Until the 1960s, the American press always spelled *Fascism* with a capital F, and used the word exclusively to describe the regimes of Hitler, Mussolini, Franco, and the like. It was only the

international left that made *fascist* a vague indictment of capitalism and the right. Already in 1937, George Orwell was complaining that the communists had reduced the word to meaninglessness: "I have heard it applied to farmers, shopkeepers, Social
Credit, corporal punishment, fox-hunting, bull-fighting, the 1922
Committee, the 1941 Committee, Kipling, Gandhi, Chiang Kai-
Shek, homosexuality, Priestley's broadcasts, Youth Hostels, astrol-
ogy, women, dogs and I do not know what else." Yet even so,
Orwell suggested that the word retained a certain core of emotional significance—to most people on the left, he said, it referred
to "something cruel, unscrupulous, arrogant, obscurantist, anti-
liberal and anti-working-class."

That was the small-f use of *fascist* that was picked up by
American radicals of the sixties, at a moment when "polariza-
tions were the common syntax [and] extremities were ordinary,"
as Todd Gitlin has put it. The charge of "fascism" became a way
of distancing yourself from the tired civilities of liberalism—the
word could stand in for any form of social control that might dis-
incline someone to work on Maggie's farm no more. When
William F. Buckley brought a defamation suit against the author
of a 1969 book for calling him a fascist, the court ruled that the
word was too vague to be actionable.

The collapse of the revolutionary movements of the sixties
temporarily bleached *fascist* of its tone of rage. Over the following decades it was mostly a jocular description for anyone who
was trying to impose rigid patterns of behavior. People talked
about fashion fascists and wine fascists, and pinned *fascistic* on
everything from anti-smoking ordinances to those annoying seat
belts that lock you in automatically when you close the car door.

Now, though, "fascist" has been revived as a political epithet.

The anger stirred up by the Iraq war and the Administration's domestic anti-terrorism programs has many leftists pulling the word out of the closet, along with tie-dye t-shirts and chants of "hey hey ho ho." An AltaVista search turns up more than 7,500 pages where "fascist" or "fascism" appears within ten words of "Ashcroft" or "Bush."

True, not everything is the same as it was in the sixties. Anti-war demonstrators may call Bush and Ashcroft fascists, but you rarely hear them yelling "fascist pigs" at the police—a sign of the restraint that both protesters and cops have learned since the bloody confrontations in Chicago in 1968.

This time around, the right has taken up the epithet as well. Sometimes that's appropriate, as when supporters of the Iraq war use "fascist" to describe Saddam Hussein's regime. Saddam's Iraq may not have been the kind of corporatist state that Mussolini and Hitler were trying to build, but it had a lot of the same substance and style as classical fascism: the militaristic nationalism, a secular religion of the state, and a government by secret police terror—not to mention grandiose public monuments and those silly high-peaked caps like the ones that German and Italian officers sported.

The only person who found anything to object to in that comparison was the Italian Prime Minister Silvio Berlusconi, who complained to British journalists that Mussolini's regime was far more benign than Saddam's. "Mussolini never killed anyone," he said—not entirely accurately. "Mussolini used to send people on vacation in internal exile." (Berlusconi later said that he had been tricked by the journalists into making the remarks while drinking a bottle of champagne "at the end of a long day, when I was very tired." He didn't withdraw the remarks, however.)

Still, it's striking that few people were calling Saddam a fascist at the time of the first Gulf War thirteen years ago. In 1990, there were only eleven stories in major newspapers and magazines where someone described Saddam's regime as fascist; over the past year there have been more than 150.

And it's more of a stretch when people, generally on the right, use phrases like "Islamo-fascist" to describe Islamic fundamentalists. The Taliban government may have been a repressive theocracy, but it wasn't particularly reminiscent of Hitler or Mussolini's regimes, which tried to make religion subordinate to the cult of the state and the leader and which made a fetish of material progress. It's as if the evils of the Taliban and bin Laden aren't sufficient to the day—we can't go after anyone now without comparing the campaign to the "good war" against Hitler, the embodiment of inexplicable evil, and everybody's favorite argument in favor of preventive war. It's part and parcel of the way *appeaser* was tacked on to anyone who had reservations about the Iraq war, in another strategic invocation of historical memory.

In fact the right has taken to using *fascist* with the reckless brio that we used to associate with Abbie Hoffman and Jerry Rubin. Rush Limbaugh has described Dick Gephardt's health care program as fascist, and a few months ago the director of the American Conservative Union called Tim Robbins a fascist for complaining that the right-wing media are stifling dissent. When Jerry Springer was considering a run for the Senate in Ohio in July, the *National Review*'s Jonah Goldberg likened his rhetoric to that of a fascist demagogue.

The right's new enthusiasm for the fascist label may be the result of the fall of Communism, which left old epithets like *pinko* and *communistic* sounding quaint and retro. (In recent years, in fact, *Communism* has grown a capital letter, even as *fascism* was losing its own—people think of Communism as a closed chapter in world history, bracketed by Lenin's arrival at Finland Station on one end and the fall of the Berlin Wall on the other.)

There was a time when the right would routinely refer to the ACLU as communist sympathizers or a communist front. That association was implicit when the elder George Bush described Michael Dukakis as "a card-carrying member of the ACLU," a phrase that echoed the way Senator McCarthy referred to members of the Communist Party. Nowadays, though, Fox News host Bill O'Reilly describes the group as a "fascist organization," which "uses their legal clout to terrorize various school districts and individuals." That's as silly as the earlier charges that the group was communist. Real fascists don't try to litigate their way to power—if they did, they wouldn't have been fascists.

But then few of the Americans who use *fascist* nowadays have much interest in dotting their historical *i*'s. Like *Big Brother* or *Orwellian*, it's a spandex specter that you can stretch over anything that smacks of excessive control and surveillance, whether it comes from the left, the right, or the seat-belt makers.

The loose use of *fascist* comes particularly easy to Americans. For most of the peoples of Europe, the word still conjures up a shameful episode that has to be lived down—or, in Berlusconi's case, excused away. But we can toss the fascist label around with easy abandon, secure in the conviction that really "it can't happen here," as Sinclair Lewis ironically titled his 1935 novel about a fascist takeover of the United States. Americans may not have a vivid sense of history, but you can count on them to reject anything if you can persuade them to picture it in a high-peaked cap.

Class Dismissed

"Class warfare" is on a roll right now. The phrase has appeared in the press more often in the month of January 2003 than it did in the whole second half of 2002, and it's on track to blow right by its previous two seasonal peaks. Those were in the summer of 2000, when Republicans were accusing Al Gore of waging class warfare in his presidential campaign, and back in 1995, when they were making the same charge about the Democratic critics of Newt Gingrich's Contract with America.

That conservatives keep coming back to the charge of "class warfare" is a sign of how well it works. Some liberals are willing to throw the phrase back at Bush—as New York Congressman Charles Rangel put it, "If this is class warfare, who started it?" But to most Americans, "class warfare" echoes too much of cloth caps and barricades. It's like something out of *Les Miz*, not *Mr. Smith Goes to Washington*.

What makes "class warfare" so alien? According to conservatives, it's because Americans reject "the politics of envy," another favorite phrase with a long pedigree—back in 1896, Theodore Roosevelt was accusing William Jennings Bryan of having "invoked the aid of mean and somber vices of envy, of hatred for the well-to-do." As David Brooks put it in a *New York Times* op-ed piece, "[In America], people vote their aspirations. . . . [We] have always had a sense that great opportunities lie just over the horizon. . . . None of us is really poor; we're just pre-rich."

Well, that's one theory—that working Americans will welcome the Bush tax proposals in hopeful anticipation of the day when they'll be living off their own stock dividends. But I suspect that the discomfort that Americans have with the notion of "class warfare" owes a lot to the way we use the word *class* itself—or rather to the way we don't use it.

It's notable that the conservatives who decry the politics of class warfare never go on to finish the thought—you never hear them talk about the virtues of "class cooperation." In fact the phrases "class warfare" and "class envy" are pretty much the only place where the word "class" occurs at all in the American conservative lexicon—I mean, when it's not preceded by "middle." If you search on the speeches and statements at the whitehouse.gov Web site you'll find fifty hits for "middle class," but none at all for "working class." You get a few more hits if you expand the search to "working families," but that's not the same thing—it's the difference between the Bunkers and the Huxtables.

Needless to say, the phrase "upper-class" doesn't appear at the whitehouse.gov site either. That phrase has pretty much disappeared from American political discourse. People may still talk about upper-class neighborhoods or the upper-class character in a movie, but you very rarely see a phrase like "upper-class voters" or "upper-class taxpayers."

The connection between "upper class" and income and power was already getting cloudy when Jay Gatsby moved to West Egg, and by now it's almost too vague to define. You could

see that in the exit polls conducted by the Voter News Service
after the 2000 presidential elections. Not surprisingly, the 29 percent of voters who described themselves as "upper middle class"
went for Bush over Gore by about a five-to-four margin. But the 4
percent of voters who described themselves as "upper class" actually voted three-to-two for Gore.

Just who were those voters, anyway? They clearly weren't just
the 4 percent at the top of the income scale—in fact, the same
exit polls showed that voters with incomes over $100,000 went
decisively for Bush. And it isn't likely they were old-style patri-
cians like the Bushes, the Auchinclosses, or the Rockefellers. That
crowd certainly didn't go three-to-two for Gore, and anyway they
don't make up anything like 4 percent of the population, which
would come to around 6 million households—a figure a lot bigger than the circulation of *Town and Country*.

In fact, those self-styled upper-class voters were probably no
different in income or social status from the ones who described
themselves as upper-middle-class. They were simply the ones
who were willing to say that an income of $100,000 a year put
them in a privileged group—something that Democrats are more
likely to own up to than Republicans are.

Conservatives like to say that class is an illusion in American
life. As David Brooks puts it, "Americans do not see society as a
layer cake, with the rich on top, the middle class beneath them
and the working class and underclass at the bottom." It makes
you wonder why people use those phrases at all. But it's significant that Brooks started that list with "the rich," rather than "the
upper class." Americans have no qualms about acknowledging a
distinction between the middle class and the working class—if
they didn't, where would that leave Roseanne or Bruce Spring-

steen? And we recognize the existence of an underclass, too, even if we usually describe it in racial or ethnic terms.

But as those exit polls showed, most Americans don't see the wealthy as a separate class. Say "upper-class" to most people and what comes to mind is Thurston Howell III, not Jack Welch. My guess is that if you asked him, Welch would be quick to describe himself as upper-middle-class, pointing out that he still prefers beer to wine.

That's the trick to all this talk of "class warfare." Middle-income Americans may be painfully aware of the gulf that separates them from the wealthy, but they don't think of those in terms of class lines. To a high-school principal making $80,000 a year, the only class difference is between herself and the school janitor, not between herself and a coupon-clipping investor. *Class* is a word that sets Americans to looking over their shoulder. I think of what my friend Bob said many years ago as we were nervously chaining up our bicycles outside a restaurant on upper Broadway in New York: "When you buy a ten-speed, the class war comes home to you."

Special Effects

As British demonstrators were organizing for yesterday's anti-Bush protests, the right-wing *Daily Mail* warned that if they damaged the relationship with America, they would damage Britain as well. "This is our closest and most reliable ally," the paper said, "tied to us by a shared commitment to freedom, by a common language and a common history, not to mention immensely important trade links."

The references to a common language are *de rigueur* whenever Britons are defending the "special relationship," a phrase that they use a lot more than we do. But historically speaking, it was the special relationship that created the common language, rather than the other way round. It wasn't inevitable that the two nations would think of themselves as speaking the same language—people often distinguish separate languages with varieties that are no more distinct than British and American are, like Dutch and Afrikaans or Norwegian and Danish. In fact, in the decades following the American Revolution, people like Adams and Jefferson argued that Americans should break off their linguistic ties with England, just as they had thrown off its political yoke. Not that we were about to switch to speaking Greek or

Fresh Air commentary, November 20, 2003

German, but over the course of time American would become a language "distinct from the rest of the world," as Noah Webster put it. And to make the point symbolically, Webster went about altering American orthography so that Americans and Englishmen would wind up writing "honor" in different ways.

It wasn't until fifty or sixty years later that the English and Americans somewhat grudgingly decided to maintain their linguistic union, like a couple that goes through a trial separation and then decides to stick it out. That realization no doubt reflected the pull of a common literary and political heritage—as Anthony Trollope wrote in 1862, "[An American] separates himself from England in politics and perhaps in affection; but he cannot separate himself from England in mental culture." But it also owed a lot to the neurotic dependencies that can bind families more closely than mere history does. If England and America didn't think of themselves as speaking the same language, the English couldn't accuse us of mangling it, and we wouldn't have the satisfaction of knowing how much our cheeky linguistic high jinks annoyed those stiff grown-ups back in the parlor.

The British have always had a high time portraying Americans as backwoods buffoons who spout a mixture of slang, malaprops, and bloated pomposities. For them, America was the source of all linguistic corruption, in something like the way that we think of California today. In 1869, the English critic G. F. Graham accused Americans of taking liberties with the language. "'slick', 'spry', and 'boss' are not English words, and we may pretty confidently expect that they will never become English."

It was around then that British critics began to use the phrase "President's English" in a mocking way. When an American news dispatch announced in 1864 that General Grant was going home to "recuperate," using the verb in a new, intransitive sense, a writer in *Punch* asked "How can people who call themselves members of the Anglo-Saxon family use such language? . . . you who owe allegiance to Her Majesty, and are in duty bound to maintain the purity of the Queen's English; consider all such English as 'Recuperate' President's English, spurious, base, villainous: pray you, avoid it."

That has been the dominant note in British commentaries on American English ever since—a mixture of affectionate condescension, ridicule, and occasionally genuine bile, particularly when relations between the two countries were strained. While the Civil War was raging in 1864, the Dean of Canterbury wrote: "Look at the process of deterioration which our Queen's English has undergone at the hands of the Americans . . . and then compare the character and history of the nation—its blunted sense of moral obligation and duty to man . . . ; and its reckless and fruitless maintenance of the most cruel and unprincipled war in the history of the world."

True, the British have usually overdrawn their depictions of American speech—Dickens rendered it so broadly in *American Notes* that Emerson felt obliged to complain that "no such conversations ever occur in this country in real life." But if no American actually talks like those caricatures, George Bush comes pretty close. British critics of Bush and his policies may make a point of saying that their beef is with the president and not the country. But it's certainly convenient that Bush fits the negative stereotype of Americans so neatly—he's a self-made straw man.

The London *Sunday Times*, which has been generally supportive of Bush, recently asked 2000 Britons which characteristics they most associate with the U.S. president. The largest proportion said he was "a danger to world peace," but that was followed closely by the adjectives "stupid" and "incoherent." And in the *Times* of London last week, the conservative columnist Matthew Parris observed not entirely approvingly that these days any English comic can get a laugh with a joke that depicts Bush as "a loud, bumptious, ignorant, crass, narrow-minded, conspiring, lethal zealot." As Parris notes, "The trouble with Bush jokes is that they are really about Americans."

Of course, a lot of people on this side of the pond think of Bush as an America joke, too. That's the price we Americans pay for the special relationship—we all have a little introjected Englishman perched on our shoulder, clucking his tongue at our ignorance and faulty grammar. And it can be embarrassing to see the flesh-and-blood embodiment of those defects sharing a platform with Tony Blair.

But nowadays Americans seem to be making less fun of Bush's linguistic derelictions, whichever side they're on. Before the September 11 attacks and the Iraq war, the president's supporters could make light of his gaffes as harmless foibles. Now even that concession seems to undercut their efforts to drape a Churchillian mantle over the man and his language. An article in *National Review* goes so far as to describe him as "speaking with Churchillian clarity." I doubt whether even the *Daily Mail* would have ventured that description for a British audience.

Bush's language has become a less important issue for his American critics, too. Not that they don't still regard him an ignorant bumpkin (or worse, a pseudo-bumpkin) who embarrasses the country, but now they're concerned that he's making America look bad in much more dangerous ways. That anger has nothing to do with the fact that Bush doesn't talk like Tony Blair—or for that matter, that Tony Blair does.

[Symbols]

A Date to Remember

Back in 1979 when I was living in Rome, the singer Francesco de Gregori had an odd hit with a kind of alternative national anthem called *Viva l'Italia*, which has since become a classic. The song is laced with an ironic affection for Italy with all its faults—the tone is more like *My Funny Valentine* than the love-it-or-leave-it swagger of our patriotic country songs or the angry repudiations of our protest music.

Viva l'Italia, it went, "plundered and betrayed...half garden and half jail...Italy with its eyes shut in the dark night, Italy unafraid." The last verse went: "Viva L'Italia, Italy of the 12th of December, Italy in its flags and Italy naked as always, Italy with its eyes open in the sad night, Italy that resists."

I had to ask an Italian friend about that reference to the 12th of December—it turned out to be the day in 1969 when neo-fascists set off bombs in Milan and Rome that killed sixteen people and wounded more than 100, initiating a long period of violence and instability. The Italians are always using dates to refer to important events. In Rome alone there are streets named May 24, September 8, September 20, February 8, October 25, and November 4, all of them commemorating various events of national significance.

Fresh Air Commentary, September 11, 2003

The Italians aren't alone in this. The French still refer to the major developments of the French revolution as the 9 Thermidor (the overthrow of Robespierre in 1794) and the 18 Brumaire (Napoleon's coup of 1799), using the names of the months in the revolutionary calendar, and they've kept up the practice for recent events. An article in *Le Monde* last week asked whether the socialists might be heading for "a new 21st of April," the date of the first round of the 2002 presidential elections when the party was eliminated by the far-right party of Jean-Marie le Pen. The Germans use "June 17" as shorthand for the uprisings against the East German communist regime in 1953, and the Portuguese use "April 25" to refer to their 1974 revolution.

As it happens, we Americans are one of the few nations who don't refer to historical events this way. There's the Fourth of July, of course, but we only use that date to refer to the annual holiday, not the approval of the Declaration of Independence by the Continental Congress in 1776. We talk about "Pearl Harbor," "V-E Day," and "the Kennedy assassination," not "December 7," "May 8," or "November 22."

September 11 is the one exception. That may be because the events of that day happened in several different places—giving the date is more compact than saying "The terrorist attacks on the World Trade Center and the Pentagon and in a plane over Pennsylvania." But even so, we seem to feel the need to assign the date a special form that's distinct from the way we refer to dates in conversation. Since the attacks, "September 11" has been steadily losing ground to "9/11." That's the way we write a date in headlines or on a check, not what we say in conversation when someone asks for our birthday. In fact for many people the "9/11" form has been detached from its calendric meaning, which is what leads them to pronounce it as "nine-one-one." That's partly due to a confusion with the police emergency number, of course. But we're never tempted to say "nine-one-one" when we're reading a date off a check stub.

Of course you could say that our reluctance to refer to events by their dates is simply a matter of avoiding ambiguity as to which year we're talking about. But people in other nations don't seem to have any problem understanding these references— "Would that be next 18 Brumaire you're talking about, or the one back in 1799?"

For the French or Italians, that's the point of referring to events as "December 12" or "April 21"—it appeals to the collective memory of a community linked by a common daily experience. You have the image of a people turning the pages of the calendar in unison and marking the important dates in red letters. It's the same sense of history that allows families to refer to the dates of birthdays and anniversaries without having to remind each other what their significance is.

That familial sense of national community comes more naturally to a homogeneous people with a history that transcends regimes and revolutions. We Americans don't really think of ourselves as a people in that sense—when we talk about "the American people," we usually continue with "are" rather than "is." That may be why we're uncomfortable with the kind of patriotism you hear in de Gregori's Italian anthem. When my sister and I talk about our relatives we can allow ourselves a tone of fond exasperation, without having to worry that anybody's going to accuse us of being anti-Nunberg.

As families go, at any rate, we Americans aren't good at remembering the dates of our anniversaries. Shortly after the Battle of Lexington and Concord in 1775, John Adams' wife Abigail wrote that the 19th of April would be "ever memorable for America as the Ides of March to Rome." But outside of Massachusetts, where Patriot's Day was regularly celebrated on April 19 until it became a moveable feast a few years ago, the only people who mark that date now are the decidedly unfamilial far-rightists who associate it with Waco and the Oklahoma City bombing. Most Americans couldn't tell you when the shot heard round the world was fired—or for that matter, by whom and at what.

That may very well be the fate of the date of the terrorist attacks of 2001, too, within a couple of generations. But in the meantime, there's something to be said for referring to the events simply as September 11, rather than with that bureaucratic-sounding 9/11. It's only two extra syllables, and it locates the events where they happened, in the middle of our daily lives.

Our Nation's Favorite Song

The events of September 11 have set everyone to rethinking the significance of patriotic symbols, but change was in the air anyway. The last time we overhauled the apparatus of patriotism was around the turn of the twentieth century. The Pledge of Allegiance was composed in 1892 by Francis Bellamy, a Boston socialist and Baptist minister. And it wasn't until 1916 that President Wilson issued an executive order that made *The Star-Spangled Banner* our official national anthem, around the same time he declared Flag Day a national holiday.

The Star-Spangled Banner is the most vulnerable of all of these symbols. People have been complaining for a long time that the song was too militaristic. During the First World War Congress criminalized singing the third stanza, with its line "Their blood has wash'd out their foul footsteps' pollution," which was held to be offensive to our British allies. And not long ago, a school board in Madison, Wisconsin, instructed schools to use only an instrumental version.

That's not entirely a fair charge—after all, those rockets and bombs were coming from the British ships that were bombarding Fort McHenry as Francis Scott Key watched helplessly from the

Fresh Air Commentary, October 26, 2001

harbor, and a song about America surviving a foreign attack should be very much *à propos* right now.

Still, a lot of people would as soon have an anthem with no war images at all. And *The Star-Spangled Banner* does have insurmountable musical deficiencies. It's fun to cheer at a baseball game when a diva hits the high note on "land of the free." But there are times when people want to be able to sing an anthem in unison without having to strain.

That may explain why people have been spontaneously adopting auxiliary anthems. During the last few weeks of the major-league season, baseball teams began playing *God Bless America* just before *Take Me Out to the Ballgame* at the seventh-inning stretch, and a lot of spectators were responding just as they do with *The Star-Spangled Banner*, standing and removing their hats. It's certainly the catchiest of all the contenders, and it would be fitting for America to have an anthem originally written as a show tune. But the title would be controversial, and most Americans would want their official anthem to be a bit mustier and more decorously phrased.

America the Beautiful has a suitable pedigree. It was composed in 1892 by a Wellesley professor named Katharine Lee Bates. The movement to make it our national anthem goes back to 1926, and has gained support since September 11. Willie Nelson closed the all-star TV benefit on September 22 by leading everyone in singing the song, and ABC News correspondent Lynn Sherr had a book high on the bestseller lists with the title *"America the Beautiful": The Stirring True Story Behind Our Nation's Favorite Song*.

The appeal of the song isn't hard to explain. *America the Beautiful* may not be a stirring hymn like *Battle Hymn of the Republic*, the only patriotic song that America has produced that could go elbow-to-elbow with the *Marseillaise* and *Deutschland Uber Alles* if it came to a showdown in Rick's cafe. But it's a pleasant tune (and more than that, when Ray Charles sings it), and it's one that we can join in on without self-consciousness.

But what really endears the song to Americans is its lyrics, with their invocations of coast-to-coast brotherhood and above all their pretty scenic pictures, like a set of old chromolithograph postcards. Even so, it troubles me to think of *America the Beautiful* as a national anthem. I'm made nervous by its overblown language, with its contorted syntax and fulsome descriptions. You have to be wary of any verses that have that many adjectives in them, particularly orotund vocables like *spacious, amber, purple,* and *fruited*—and *beautiful,* for that matter, which is usually something better implied than said.

This isn't just a stylistic quibble. That overwriting is typical of the late-nineteenth-century sentimentalization of a vanishing rural America, and the fear that urbanization and industrialization were eroding traditional American values. (That notion is picked up in later stanzas, where Bates complains that the "banner of the free" is being stained by "selfish gain" and hopes for an age of "nobler men" to "keep once again thy whiter jubilee.") Modern Americans can easily sympathize with those themes, given our own concerns about the threatened environment. But, now as then, it puts the essence of the country far from the daily lives that most of us live. As a kid in Manhattan, I remember singing about purple mountains and waves of grain and thinking that America must be a distant place, somewhere out beyond Jersey. And Bates's sublime landscape has no more to do with the country that most Americans inhabit now, a land of spacious parking lots and amber traffic signals.

Granted, we all love our purple mountains, along with our golden valleys, redwood forests, wheat fields waving, and dust clouds blowing, not to mention our fogs lifting, a particular favorite here in San Francisco. But any country can make its landscape the focus of a national anthem. The Swiss sing about the Alps going bright with splendor; the Czechs sing about water bubbling across the meadows and pinewoods rustling amongst the crags; the Brazilians sing about the sound of the sea and the light of heaven. And the Syrian anthem begins with a remarkable entomological figure: "Syria's plains are towers in the heights. . . . A land resplendent with brilliant suns . . . almost like a sky centipede."

Anthems like those are appropriate for nations that have no essential commitment to a particular form of government: Landscapes don't have any politics, after all. But the American experiment was supposed to be different; our patriotism is for a nation, not a land. No other country tells its story as the history of a single regime, and that point ought to figure prominently in whatever anthem we sing.

There's a parallel between the swelling popularity of *America the Beautiful* and the Administration's choice of *homeland security* rather than *domestic security* to describe the office headed by Governor Ridge. It's easy to understand what they were getting at, given the shock of an attack on American soil. But even though *homeland* is a perfectly good English word, up to now we've never used it to describe our own country. It has an alien sound, like the German *Heimat*—it's the word we use for peoples who feel an ancestral connection to a particular plot of ground. Whereas the idea of America isn't that it's a place that people come from but a place that they come to. The Germans and Palestinians and Kurds and Ukrainians have homelands; we just have a nation and a flag.

The Last Refuge
of Scoundrels and Other People

"Peace is patriotic"—I always want to read that slogan as meaning "peace IS SO patriotic," a response to the charge that peace advocates don't have the interests of the country at heart. But then *patriotism* is a word that exists to put people on the defensive. After all, we don't have everyday words for love of one's family or loyalty to one's friends. If we feel the need for a word for devotion to one's country, it's only to imply a contrast with those whose who lack that feeling.

Things were different when *patriot* acquired its modern sense in the seventeenth century, as a name for those who took the part of Parliament against the British monarchy, whose European connections were suspect. Monarchists like Dryden used the word in a derisory way: "Never was Patriot yet, but was a Fool."

By the eighteenth century, though, the love of one's country was coming to be an unarguable civic virtue. Boswell no sooner reported Samuel Johnson's famous declaration that "patriotism is the last refuge of a scoundrel" than he felt the need to defend the remark. Johnson, he said, "did not mean a real and generous love of our country, but that pretended patriotism which so many . . . have made a cloak for self-interest."

The New York Times Week in Review, April 13, 2003

Over the centuries, moral philosophers have wrestled with the fact that patriotism is always a kind of bias, a disposition to favor one's own nation beyond what the objective facts would warrant. As Max Eastman wrote in 1906, "If one were loyal to one's nation only because it was good and true . . . one would not be loyal to any nation, but to truth and goodness. The idea of patriotism would have no place either in our dictionaries or our lives."

That kernel of irrationality at the heart of patriotism has always been troublesome for Americans. For other nations, patriotism is basically a question of loyalty to the land of one's birth—*patrie, patria, Vaterland*—however it happens to be governed. But Americans don't have words like those to describe the objects of our patriotic attachment, or at least, not until the Teutonic-sounding "homeland" entered the national lexicon. We don't have a fatherland, only an uncle, and Americans have always tried to justify their love of him by citing the national devotion to liberty and fairness. It's as if we can't simply be attached to the land where our fathers died; we have to explain that it's the land of the pilgrims' pride, as well.

That helps to explain why others see Americans as prone to obtrude their national pride so readily. Alexis de Tocqueville complained that "It is impossible to conceive a more troublesome or more garrulous patriotism; it wearies even those who are disposed to respect it."

It's that need to justify national pride that has traditionally tied discussions of patriotism here to the notion of Americanism, as a name for the doctrines and qualities that make our nation exceptional. True, Americanism has been the refuge of quite as many scoundrels as patriotism itself. Whitman warned against those who "are using the great word Americanism without yet feeling the first aspiration of it." And in *Main Street*, Sinclair Lewis listed "One Hundred Per Cent Americanism" among the clichés of the patriotic stump orator, along with "Bountiful Harvest" and "Alien Agitators."

But Americanism was also a touchpoint for progressives and radicals. Americanization programs for immigrants were often the benign twin of early twentieth-century nativism; striking workers in the 1930s carried American flags on the picket lines. The American Communist Party chief, Earl Browder, famously declared that "communism is twentieth-century Americanism."

It wasn't until the Cold War that Americanism became the exclusive property of the right, particularly when the House Committee on Un-American Activities made "un-Americanism" a synonym for every sort of left-wing activity. In the end, *Americanism* was an unintended victim of McCarthyism. After that period the word virtually disappeared from the American political lexicon.

But American patriotism was most thoroughly transformed in the 1960s, when antiwar radicals repudiated American exceptionalism in tantrums of flag-burning. True, the flag-burners were always a small minority in the antiwar movement, and in fact the American flags at antiwar rallies greatly outnumbered Vietcong ones. But from then on, patriotism became largely a matter of defending contested symbols like the flag and the Pledge of Allegiance; for the first time in modern history, the flag itself acquired an explicitly partisan meaning. By 1984, Ronald Reagan could simply assume that the composer of a song called *Born in the U.S.A.* would be a like-minded Republican. "I have not got a clue about Springsteen's politics, if any," George Will wrote approvingly if incuriously, "but flags get waved at his concerts."

You can see the shift in the declining use of the noun *patriot*. It's still found in the names of banks, newspapers, sports teams, insurance companies, missiles, and the like, not to mention the U.S.A. Patriot Act. But when it comes to describing living people, *patriot* is outnumbered by *patriotic* by ten to one. The first is a matter of actions, the second a matter of attitude and style.

Often, in fact, modern patriotism doesn't come down to much more than consumer preference. The founder of the Hummer Owners Group recently described the vehicle as "a symbol of what we all hold so dearly above all else." Or as another Hummer owner said, the troops "aren't out there in Audi A4's."

At the same time, the traditional symbols of patriotism are treated now with a casualness that would once have been considered more appropriate for sports emblems. In 1968, Abbie Hoffman was arrested for wearing an American flag shirt to a HUAC hearing. Now pro-war demonstrators show up wearing American flag T-shirts, belt buckles, bandannas, halters, and jumpsuits. Take that together with the demonstrators' chants of "U.S.A., U.S.A." and it can be hard to tell a patriotic demonstration from a gathering of Oakland Raiders fans.

That slogan "Peace is patriotic" is an indication of the recent willingness of progressives and liberals to invoke the substantive values of Americanism, like the tradition of liberty and the constitutional sanctity of dissent. But since the 1960s, liberals have been skittish about embracing the symbolic manifestations of patriotism. You can see that diffidence in the anti-war movement's adoption of "peace flags," American flags whose stars are re-arranged in the form of the peace sign. The design makes its point and is hardly disrespectful by modern standards, but it seems an unnecessary qualification—what's wrong with Old Glory as it is?

That's partly just a stylistic aversion, particularly now that the flag has become a fashion statement for the right. But it also reflects a distrust of the emotional connotations of symbols like the flag, and perhaps a suspicion of the moral basis of patriotism itself—the idea, as the eighteenth-century English radical William Godwin put it, that there's a "magic in the pronoun *my*." Yet the anti-war movement presumes that very connection when it argues that dissent is patriotic, with the implication that we Americans must feel a special obligation to demur when we disagree with the policies of our own government.

And a love of flag and country doesn't entail a mindless jingoism. Most Americans can identify with the patriotic pride of the young marine who draped the American flag over the head of the statue of Saddam Hussein in downtown Baghdad, in what instantly became the defining image of American—hardly "coalition"—triumph. But many people also realized just how problematic a gesture that was, and how imprudent and simplistic uncritical flag-waving can be as a response to the challenges that are facing the country. That's as it should be; the tension between emotional and reflective expressions of patriotism has always been a defining trait of Americanism. Come to think of it, now that the memories of HUAC have receded, it might be a good time to revive that word.

Pledge Break

The oddest thing about the Pledge of Allegiance is that people can take its wording so seriously even as they find it charming that children are always getting it wrong. Everybody can cite some second-grader's winsome misconstruction of the text: "I led a pigeon to the flag"; "and to the republic for witches' dance"; "one naked individual." For that matter, nobody seems to mind that even older students are pretty fuzzy on the meanings of words like *allegiance*, *republic*, and *indivisible*. (*Slate*'s Timothy Noah calculated the readability of the pledge at the ninth-grade level, and even that is misleadingly low, since the Flesch-Kincaid scale that Noah used wasn't designed to take into account the Pledge's singularly Victorian turns of phrase.)

In fact it's often said that the very obscurity of the pledge is what makes the phrase "under God" constitutionally unobjectionable. In 1984, Justice William Brennan described the phrase as a form of "ceremonial deism," which has "lost through rote repetition any significant religious content." That argument came up a lot in criticisms of the recent Ninth Circuit decision banning the words "under God." *Newsday* dismissed the pledge as a "harmless civic recitation" and the *Washington Post*'s Marc Fisher wrote that

Fresh Air Commentary, July 8, 2002

"God's name is just a frill, a space-filler in the unthinking torrent of much daily conversation." To hear some people tell it, you might conclude that there's not much difference between saying "one nation under God" and "one nation, by God!"

But if the pledge is merely a "harmless civic recitation," why the torrent of invective over the Ninth Circuit's decision, to the point where some op-ed trombones were comparing it with a straight face to the September 11 attacks? Columnist Cal Thomas said the court had "inflicted on this nation what many will conclude is a greater injury than that caused by the terrorists." (Where are the moral equivalence police when you need them?)

True, the pledge isn't the only obscurely worded patriotic text that can evoke strong feelings. *The Star-Spangled Banner* is famously unparsable—how many people could tell you with confidence what ramparts are or why anyone was watching them? But the pledge is the only one of these texts that was actually written for recitation by schoolchildren.

Still, Bellamy made no concessions to the linguistic limitations of his young audience. The words "I pledge allegiance" were an allusion to the oath of allegiance to the Union that many southerners were required to sign before their political rights were restored after the Civil War—a reference that was galling to some southerners, along with the business about "one nation indivisible." But none of those words would have had much meaning to schoolchildren in the 1890s, three decades after the war had ended. Nor would they have been able to make much sense of Bellamy's original wording of the end of the pledge: "with liberty, fraternity, and equality for all," a phrase that the sponsors rejected as too radical, and too French.

Granted, that was an age that delighted in high-blown patriotic language—late-nineteenth-century schoolchildren were expected to memorize and declaim orations like Patrick Henry's "Give me liberty" and Daniel Webster's "Against Hayne." But the pledge persevered even after those exercises and elaborate patriotic pageants and rituals were dropped from the curriculum, and in fact its syntax grew more convoluted over the next sixty years. Bellamy had originally written "I pledge allegiance to my flag." But in 1924 that was changed, over his objection, to the more unwieldy "the flag of the United States of America"—this at the urging of the Daughters of the American Revolution, who were worried that the ambiguity of "my flag" might offer a loophole to immigrants who wanted to maintain their allegiance to the flags of Italy or the Second International. (You can't be too careful.)

The pledge became even more opaque when "under God" was added in 1954, so as to underscore the difference between godfearing us and godless them. Whether or not you agree with the sentiment of the addendum, it's hard to defend its syntax. For one thing, the interpolation leaves the modifier *indivisible* dangling at a remove from the word *nation*. And more to the point, it isn't at all clear what "under God" is supposed to mean. The phrase was taken from the Gettysburg Address, but Lincoln used it as an adverb—"this nation, under God, shall have a new birth of freedom" (that is, *under God* modifies *have*). But in the pledge, *under God* was somehow changed to an adjective, which leaves its meaning up for grabs. Is that the *under* of "under heaven," the *under* of "under a monarch," or the *under* of "under orders"? Does it mean that we believe in God or that we're subject to Him or that we have His personal attention? It's anyone's guess, since the phrase isn't used that way anywhere else in the English language. But then that vagueness is probably what commends the phrase in the first place—what better way to signal the doctrinal neutrality of the state than to express our official deism so obscurely?

Helpful schoolteachers sometimes try to explain the pledge to their charges in words that they can understand: "I promise to be true to the symbol of my country, the United States, a single country where people believe in a supreme being and which can't be split apart. . . ." But there wouldn't be much support for simplifying the official wording of the pledge, much less for replacing it with a more meaningful text like Lincoln's Second Inaugural. We like the pledge as it is, in all its turgid opacity. All that talk about "harmless civic recitations" gets the pledge wrong. Because there is a point to having children gather in collective acquiescence to sentences they don't really comprehend. As Eric Hobsbawm once observed, patriotic rituals are invented to provide the emotional signs of membership in a club, not its bylaws. "Dah-dah-dah *flag*, dah-dah-dah *America*, dah-dah-dah *God*, dah-dah-dah *liberty* . . . "—it's Americanism scored for rhythm band.

[**Media Words**]

Rush Limbaugh's Plurals

"I think some of the sports media is influenced in their opinion of his performance by their desire for a black quarterback to do well. And now that—that—my friends, is the point of this."

That was Rush Limbaugh on his radio show on October 1, 2003, explaining the comments he had made a few days earlier on ESPN's *NFL Today*, when he said that the media were going easy on Philadelphia Eagles's quarterback Donovan McNabb because of his race. A few days later, the controversy over the remarks obliged Limbaugh to resign from his new post as a television football analyst (though the story was rapidly eclipsed by the revelations about his drug use).

Keep your eye on that plural vocative "my friends." It helps to explain a curious feature of the incident: Why was everybody up in arms about a remark that wouldn't have raised an eyebrow if Limbaugh had made it on his regular radio broadcast?

True, Limbaugh was talking on a sports show, not a political broadcast. But then ESPN had hired him in the hope that his talents as a controversialist would liven up the show, and indeed, its ratings rose 10 percent after he began to appear. And while his remark may have had racial overtones, it wasn't racist in

itself—and certainly not in the same league as some of the things
he has said on his radio show, like telling an African-American
caller to "take that bone out of your nose and call me back."

Whether or not the comment warranted Limbaugh's departure from the program, the incident drove home once again that
you can say things on radio that you simply can't say on TV. In
July of 2003, Michael Savage was abruptly yanked from his weekend talk slot on MSNBC after he addressed an unidentified caller
as "you sodomite" and said he should "get AIDS and die." Yet
Savage raises scarcely a public ripple when he effervesces along
similar lines to his 5 million radio listeners.

Some people have tried to justify the difference in standards
by saying that listeners to radio talk shows tend to be partisans
who know what to expect from the hosts, while TV seems to be
aimed at a general audience. TV, we like to say, comes into our
living rooms, whereas talk radio is a vice that we indulge in in the
privacy of our cars.

That distinction is more a matter of perception than of reality. But there is a difference in the way the two media present
themselves to the public, which is implicit in the forms of address
that each of them uses. Apart from formulaic openings like
"Good evening, everyone," television news shows almost always
address their viewers in the singular: "Up next, protecting yourself from Internet scams." "Should the tires on your car have an
expiration date?" Or think of the famous scene in *Network* where
Peter Finch, playing a newscaster, tells his audience: "I want you
to go to the window, open it, stick your head out and yell: 'I'm as
mad as hell, and I'm not going to take this anymore!'"
Note—your head, not your heads.

That's the same convention used in print. A newspaper financial columnist would hardly advise readers that "It's a good time

to buy yourselves new cars." And the confiding tone of *Jane Eyre* would be severely ruptured if Charlotte Brontë had begun the conclusion with the sentence, "Readers, I married him."

The singular presupposes a one-to-one relationship between a speaker and an addressee. It's the picture implicit in the word "broadcast" itself, which originally referred to scattering seeds by hand in the hope that some of them would find a favorable landing place. In that sense, as the critic Raymond Williams once said, it's something of a misnomer to describe television as a mass medium. For the most part, television news speaks to each of us as an individual citizen, even if the communication is reproduced in millions of places at the same time.

But like other radio talk-show hosts, Limbaugh prefers the plural: "I'll tell you what, folks ..."; " You Dittoheads out there ...," "Some of you may say ..." That form of address suggests the presence of a group of people—an audience, rather than just a listenership. It has the effect of creating an "us" and a "them"; it turns radio into a kind of crowd phenomenon like a concert, where individual judgments are subordinated to solidarity with the group.

The image of a group of addressees is well adapted to the coy pomposity of Limbaugh's radio persona—he plays his audience like a comic working the room. And it helps to explain why the remarks he makes on the radio don't engender the same public indignation as the far milder things he says on TV. It would be like getting shirty about the content of a Margaret Cho performance—if it bothers you, don't buy a ticket.

Right-wing radio commentators don't have a monopoly on this device. You hear it from disc jockeys, shock jocks, sports talk hosts, and even from some of the left-wing hosts on the Pacifica stations (though not on NPR, where the plural is generally reserved for requests like "Send us your letters"). Limbaugh and his fellow conservatives have merely been adroit at using the device to create a setting for political entertainment—not surprising, given that many of them cut their teeth in other radio formats.

But the choice of a form of address isn't inherent in the media themselves. You occasionally hear those plurals on TV children's shows, and they've begun to show up in the mouths of hosts on Fox News. "You guys have made me the poster boy for the American dream," Bill O'Reilly told his audience in a recent commentary segment. If that intimate tone works anywhere on TV, it's on Fox News—the closest thing on TV to the political talk stations on radio, fair-and-balanced wall-to-wall.

There was a time when radio talk shows had the same public status that we now accord to TV. In the 1930s, the "radio priest" Father Charles Coughlin provoked repeated national controversies with weekly broadcasts in which he praised the Nazi regime and charged that "International Jewry" was responsible for Bolshevism and the Depression. Coughlin's audience ultimately reached 16 million, proportionately far larger than Limbaugh's 20 million listeners today, even though the NBC radio network and a number of local stations banned him from their airwaves. (In 1938, the management of New York City's WMCA announced that carrying the broadcasts was not in the public interest, because they brought "religious or racial strife and dissension to America.")

Nowadays, of course, most of Coughlin's views would be beyond the pale even for AM. But a modern-day Father Coughlin would have pretty wide leeway to be offensive or crude, so long as he stuck to radio and was careful to address his listeners as "youse." That's the modern standard of media civility—you can say pretty much anything you want, as long as you keep it to the 20 million like-minded people in the room.

The Politics of Polysyndeton

The stylistic differences between the left and right aren't just a question of the words they use, but the tunes they sing them to. Take a piece by the *Wall Street Journal*'s Peggy Noonan on the resurgence of patriotism, or as she calls it, "the simple idea of the goodness of loving America." The nation that won the war had nothing to do with big-city elites, she says; it was "a bigger America and a realer one—a healthy and vibrant place full of religious feeling and cultural energy and Bible study and garage bands and sports-love and mom-love and sophistication and normality."

And and *and* and *and* and *and* ... —that repetition of conjunctions is what rhetoricians call polysyndeton. It does a lot of work for Noonan here. Each of those *and*'s implies an "and not"—an opposition to the urban cosmopolitans who don't have religious feeling, don't study the Bible, don't love their moms, and don't have garage bands, most likely because they don't have garages. They're the people Noonan describes as the "intellectuals, academics ... , and leftist mandarins," not to mention the "local clever people who talk loudly in restaurants." (And they would be ... ?)

Then too, the *and*'s flatten the differences among all those unlike things—replace the conjunctions with commas, and all of a sudden the thought emerges in all its vacuous incoherence: "a place full of religious feeling, cultural energy, Bible study, garage bands, sports-love, mom-love, sophistication, and normality."

Noonan's prose often dances to that rhythm. "It was daring and brilliant and brave" ... "You want to really feel it and experience it and smell it and touch it and thank God for it" ... "It's hard to describe how exciting and moving and idealism-inspiring it was" ... "now, in 2002, with so much more equality and working together and living next door to each other and sending our kids to the same schools and Boy Scout meetings."

But then a lot of columnists use this device, particularly the ones on the right. From David Horowitz: "They hate you because you are democratic, and tolerant and unbelieving. They hate you because you are Christians....And they hate you because you are Hindus and Buddhists and secularists and Jews." From David Brooks: "America does seem at once crass and materialistic and strong and indomitable." From Jack Kemp: "Bob Dole has...unfurled our banner of growth and opportunity and hope and cultural renewal." It's as if most of the American right was off at a retreat on the day when the rest of freshman English class was covering the serial comma.

William Bennett writes that "Real fatherhood means love and commitment and sacrifice and a willingness to share responsibility and not walking away from one's children." And Michelle Malkin writes in a letter to American soldiers: "You hail from Middletown and Middleboro and Greenville and Redding and Thousand Oaks and Maple Tree." (And South Central and the Bronx, she might have added, or is this another garage-band thing?)

True, you won't hear this rhythm from conservatives like William F. Buckley, George Will, or William Safire, none of them writers who are given to flights of gush. And there are liberal writers with a weakness for the device, like the tirelessly expansive Molly Ivins. ("Being a congenital optimist, I naturally believe all this will change, that we will have another surge of progressivism and reform and hell-raising and fun and justice.") But even so, this pattern is about five times as likely to occur on conservative sites like townhall.com or in *National Review* as in liberal publications like the *Nation* or the *American Prospect*.

It isn't as if polysyndeton has an inherently political meaning, or any inherent meaning at all. It has roots that go back to King Lear's "we'll live, And pray, and sing, and tell old tales, and laugh / At gilded butterflies, and hear poor rogues / Talk of court news," and it has been used since then by writers from Lewis Carroll to Bob Dylan ("And I'll tell it and think it and speak it and breathe it, And reflect it from the mountain so all souls can see it . . ."). But the pattern has a particular cadence in American writing, where it signals plenitude and immediacy, as if you're laying down your thoughts one scoop after another. It bubbles up whenever people are waxing sentimental about dogs, baseball, or the English language—particularly about the English language, I've noticed. And it's a staple of eulogies and of course book blurbs, where it's often compounded by alliteration—"wise and winsome and witty and warm."

Ultimately, this is just another one of the things we can blame Walt Whitman for, along with all the writers who mimicked his voluble spontaneity. ("The early lilacs became part of this child, / And grass and white and red morning-glories, and white and red clover, and the song of the phoebe-bird, / And the Third-month lambs and the sow's pink-faint litter, and the mare's foal and the cow's calf . . . ,")

But it's not likely that Peggy Noonan picked this up directly from Whitman, much less from Allen Ginsberg or Gary Snyder, who were fond of Whitmanesque phrasing. If you listen to Noonan's sentences, you hear another, even more familiar voice:

> Just remember this, Mr. Potter: that this rabble you're talking about, they do most of the working and paying and living and dying in this community. Well, is it too much to have them work and pay and live and die in a couple of decent rooms and a bath?

> No, but you . . . you . . . you're thinking of this place all wrong. As if I had the money back in a safe. The money's not here. Your money's in Joe's house . . . right next to yours. And in the Kennedy house, and Mrs. Macklin's house, and a hundred others.

It's all there in Frank Capra's *It's a Wonderful Life*. It's the pattern that playwrights and screenwriters of the thirties and forties used when they wanted to evoke the artless wisdom of the common man—you think of the scene in *Mr. Smith Goes to Washington*, where James Stewart says:

> Get up there with that lady that's up on top of this Capitol dome, that lady that stands for liberty. Take a look at this country through her eyes if you really want to see something. . . . There's no place out there for graft, or greed, or lies, or compromise with human liberties.

That's what Noonan and the others are aiming for with this pattern—the rhythm of the simple feelings that are obvious to everyone but the clever people who make life too complicated. But the device is apt to sound a bit more calculated and self-conscious when you run into it in the *Wall Street Journal*, particularly in an age as knowing as ours is. Back in Capra's time, people didn't make it a point of pride to be in touch with their feelings, or dwell on the simplicity of their ideas. Reading Noonan's column, I kept thinking of the recent remake of Capra's *Mr. Deeds Goes to Town*, with Adam Sandler in the Gary Cooper role.

At the end of her piece, Noonan says, "Is this corny? Too bad." Well, no. Capra was corny, and so were Robert Riskin and Nunnally Johnson and Jo Swerling and Sidney Buchman and Clifford Odets and Robert Sherwood, even if they were clever and lived in big cities and didn't go to Bible-study classes and talked too loudly in restaurants. But what Noonan does isn't corny, it's kitsch.

The Speech That Turns Mere Presidents Into Talk Show Hosts

"Every year, by law and by custom, we meet here to consider the state of the union." The beginning of President Bush's 2003 State of the Union speech echoed the phrases that Ronald Reagan was fond of using in the exordiums to his annual addresses: "In keeping with time-honored tradition"; "a constitutional duty as old as our republic itself."

Other presidents haven't usually bothered to make those observations, which would hardly come as news to the assembled legislators to whom the speech is ostensibly addressed. But Reagan understood that the occasion was really contrived for other ears—and that its effectiveness as television would be all the greater if it seemed to be a tradition that wasn't fashioned with the tube in mind.

"By law and by custom"—well, yes and no. The Constitution says only that the president "shall from time to time give to the Congress Information of the State of the Union." And while Washington and Adams made annual addresses to Congress, the practice lapsed with Jefferson, who compared the address to a "speech from the throne," a symptom of the Federalists' dangerous desire "to draw over us...the forms of the British Government."

The New York Times Week in Review, February 2, 2003

Jefferson's misgivings were still very much on people's minds when Woodrow Wilson resurrected the annual address in 1913. Senator John Sharp Williams, a Mississippi Democrat, derided Wilson's speech as "a cheap and tawdry imitation of the pomposities and cavalcadings of monarchial countries." Those criticisms weren't entirely stilled until after World War II, when Congress came to accept the speech as a presidential prerogative that should be received with respectful civility. By 1956 the political scientist Richard E. Neustadt could note "the almost total absence nowadays of vocal criticism or surprise at annual presentations of the president's program."

State of the Union addresses have been broadcast since Calvin Coolidge's 1923 speech was carried over the radio. Harry S. Truman's 1947 speech was the first to be telecast. And Lyndon B. Johnson moved the address to prime time in 1965. But it was one thing to televise the speech and another to turn it into a television show. The credit for that transformation goes to President Reagan, who signaled the new order in 1982 when he pointed to the gallery to honor Lenny Skutnik, the man who had dived into the icy Potomac to save a woman after a plane crash. That was the precedent for the bathetic "Skutnik moments" that have punctuated the addresses ever since, as well as for seeding the gallery with military leaders, foreign dignitaries, and ordinary citizens whom the TV cameras can cut to to dramatize the president's message in human terms.

More important, the 1982 speech demonstrated Reagan's realization that once the audience in the chamber was made a visible participant in the occasion, television viewers would settle into the familiar role they assume with every other kind of television talk, from *Oprah* to *Firing Line* to the local happy-talk news show—as the privileged onlookers for whom the exchange is really being transacted.

The effects on the language of the speeches have been dramatic. In 1956, Dwight D. Eisenhower described his program in dry and unemotional language directed at the legislators themselves.

> It is expected that more than $12 billion will be expended in 1955 for the development of land, water and other resources; control of floods, and navigation and harbor improvements; construction of roads, schools and municipal water supplies, and disposal of domestic and industrial wastes.

After Reagan, there would be no more plodding sentences like that one. Now the president's object is to characterize his program in stirring terms that make a coded appeal to his own constituents, but which are vague enough to land with the television audience—and which will command a deferential reception by the opposing party's members, who are obliged by the rules of the genre to respect the pretense of a direct address.

It makes for a kind of political Simon Says, as the opposition tries to decide whether to respond politely to the superficially bland appeals of the address or more truculently to their coded messages. "Instead of bureaucrats and trial lawyers and HMOs we must put doctors and nurses and patients back in charge of American medicine." Representatives Pelosi and Gephardt could greet that line with a disdainful look, recognizing the proposal to limit the legal responsibilities of health care providers. But Democrats in less safe seats would as soon not have to explain those niceties to their constituents or risk looking sulky on television.

James Fallows, a speechwriter for President Jimmy Carter, observed once that the effectiveness of the State of the Union speech has less to do with what the president says than with the repeated applause in an impressive setting. That's why the speech always raises the president's standing in the polls. But the ceremony wouldn't be nearly so effective if it actually appeared to be a made-for-TV event. Hence the importance of those invocations of custom at the beginning of Reagan's and the younger Bush's addresses, which suggest that the form and language of the speech are really dictated by the president's traditional role.

Like Jefferson, viewers today may see in this dangerous monarchial tendencies. But the British monarch's annual speech from the throne makes an explicit reference to the limits of the sovereign's power. It begins when the royal usher knocks on the door of the House of Commons, which is slammed in the official's face in a reminder that no sovereign is permitted to enter the Commons. The present-day State of the Union speech wouldn't have any place for a ritual that seems so churlish (a term derived from the Old English word for peasant). The president delivering his address isn't like a monarch, whose dutifully respectful reception is conditioned on the hard-won limitation of her temporal powers. He's something much more commanding than that—the host of his own television special—and refractory subjects can display their disagreement only by sitting on their hands.

I Seeing the News Today, Oh Boy

Every new form of journalism announces itself with a new syntax. In the mass-circulation dailies of the 1870s, Joseph Pulitzer and William Randolph Hearst gave us the compressed urgency of the modern newspaper headline. In the 1920s, *Time* magazine dramatized events with pert new coinings like *socialite*, *cinemactor*, and *politricks*, and with the inversions that Wolcott Gibbs parodied famously as "Backwards ran sentences until reeled the mind." Later, television news programs heightened the immediacy of electronic coverage with the pointer words that linguists call deictics—the "Now this" style that Chevy Chase parodied as "Here now the news."

So it's notable that the all-news networks have begun to recite their leads to a new participial rhythm: "In North Dakota, high winds making life difficult; the gusts reaching 60 m.p.h." ... "A Big Apple accident, two taxicabs plowing into crowds of shoppers." Call the new style Inglish. Fox News Channel and CNN have adopted it wholesale, and it's increasingly audible on network news programs as well.

The odd thing is that not even the newscasters seem to have a clear idea of what they're doing, or why. A *NewsHour with Jim*

Lehrer feature described the style as one of "dropping most verbs, putting everything in the present tense." But cable news reporters don't actually drop any verbs except "to be," and that only in sentences like "President Bush in Moscow." And those participles like "plowing" aren't in the present tense—they don't have any tense at all.

What Inglish really leaves out is all tenses, past, present, or future, and with them any helping verbs they happen to fall on—not just *be*, but *have* and *will*. Some people have suggested that the style suggests the language of captions, but it's used for past and future events as well. Newscasters used to say, "The Navy has used the island for sixty years but will cease its tests soon." On CNN or Fox, that comes out as "The Navy using the island for sixty years but ceasing its tests soon."

What's the point of this? The *NewsHour* called it "an abbreviated language unique to time-pressed television correspondents," and others point to the need to shoehorn as many stories as possible into a brief space. But a sense of urgency is not exactly what comes to mind when you watch the cable news shows, which seem so hard-put to fill those endless hours that they're driven to recycle an endless stream of trivia every half-hour: "Zsa Zsa Gabor no longer breathing with a respirator" ... "Ozzie and Sharon getting ready to say 'I do' all over again" ... "J-Lo firing her hairdresser after an Oscar flap." And for shoehorning purposes, the new syntax doesn't actually save any time—sometimes, in fact, it makes sentences longer. "Bush met with Putin" is one syllable shorter than "Bush meeting with Putin."

Broadcasters don't seem to realize how bizarre the new style sounds. Fox newscaster Shepherd Smith called it "people speak" and explained, "It's about how would I tell this story if I were telling it to a friend on a street corner." But that must be a pretty exotic intersection, if Smith's homeys are saying things like "My car in the shop. The brakes needing relining."

Michael Kinsley suggested that the new style is drawn from the conventions of newspaper headlines. But Inglish is actually the exact opposite of headlinese. For one thing, it doesn't omit pronouns and articles the way headlines do. If a flasher shows up at a presidential dinner, the next day's paper reports it as "Man Exposes Self at White House." On the news stations, that comes out as "A man exposing himself at the White House," which is a rather different take on the affair.

More important, headlines don't omit tenses so much as adapt them to the singular point of view of the daily news. "Buffett Buys Ad Companies" refers to an event that happened yesterday, "Buffett Bought Ad Companies" to a past event that came to light yesterday, and "Buffett to Buy Ad Companies" to a future event that was announced yesterday. That daily reference point is absent on the all-news shows, where those headlines all reduce to a tenseless "Buffett Buying Omnicom."

There's a logic to this. "The news of the day" is a notion ill-suited to news networks with peripatetic anchor desks that broadcast around the clock, adding and deleting items like top–40 stations with a high-turnover playlist. "Here now the news"—that isn't something you're likely to hear on CNN or Fox. Without a "here" and "now" there can't be "the news," measuring out daily life.

"After a night's sleep the news is as indispensable as the breakfast," Thoreau wrote sarcastically in 1854, about the time people began to use the phrase "the news" to refer to the bundle of information that's dumped on the public's doorstep on a daily basis.

That ritual of daily news consumption was a "mass ceremony," as the political scientist Benedict Anderson described it, which shaped the sense of community essential to national consciousness.

But "the news of the day" was never more than a convenient fiction, and one that the all-news broadcasters and the Internet have made it increasingly hard to sustain. So the slogans and catch-phrases change. Traditional purveyors of news referred to their product with the definite article: "All the news that's fit to print," "Here now the news." But in the slogans of the all-news outlets, the article is conspicuously absent, which reduces news to a kind of yard goods: "All news all the time"; "News at your speed"; "News when you want it."

News becoming a lot more like life, just one damn thing after another.

Roil Pain

A journalist friend asked me if I had noticed that the verb *roil* was becoming more common in the newspapers. Not surprisingly, as soon as she pointed it out I started noticing it all over the place. On one day in May of 2002, there were stories in *The New York Times* mentioning the factors that were roiling the British rail system and the roiling political context of the game of soccer. And the same day's *San Francisco Chronicle* had a story about anti-government protests that were roiling the eastern region of Algeria and a business page reference to the roiling electricity market, not to mention a headline describing Eminem as the Roiling Rapper.

There's nothing new about *roil*—it has been around since Shakespeare's time as a slightly recondite synonym for "churn up" or "perturb." But when I did a search in a collection of major newspapers, it turned out the verb is more than nine times as frequent now as it was twenty years ago, even when you correct for the changing size of the database—in fact it's up 30 percent in just the last year. That's a remarkable pop, all the more since there's no external reason for it—it isn't as if the world is nine times more turbulent than it was in 1982. But then *roil* was tailor-made

Fresh Air Commentary, June 3, 2002

for recycling as a newspaper vogue word—a bit recherché and poetic, but not so obscure that readers can't pick up a general sense of disruption. It's a particular favorite of headline writers—not surprising, given that it only has four letters, two of them skinny ones. "Migrant Pickers Roil Watermelon Capital," "Anger and Isolation Roil Israeli Arabs," or "Greenspan Remarks Roil Markets"—the stock markets alone account for about 15 percent of all the roilees in the press. But reporters use the verb in all sorts of stories, and in all sorts of ways. Sometimes *roil* seems to be a synonym for *rile* or *roll*, or even *reel*, as in "The mind roils." But then, a certain murkiness of meaning seems just about right for *roil*.

You don't hear *roil* a lot in everyday conversation. It isn't really a word of American English at all—it belongs to the patois of that exotic alter-America that we read about in the newspapers, a world populated by strongmen, fugitive financiers, and troubled teens, where ire is always being fueled until violence flares, spawning hatred and stirring fears until hopes are dashed. The Associated Press's Jack Cappon once imagined how it would sound if ordinary people actually used journalese in their conversation over the backyard fence:

> "Joe, my concern has been escalating for weeks. What's triggering our area youths, who keep sparking confrontations?"
> "Well, Bill, they certainly shattered the stillness of this affluent neighborhood with their drug-related pre-dawn rampage."

This is a venerable dialect. It has been around ever since the mass circulation penny newspapers first appeared around a hundred and fifty years ago—the garish, sensational dailies that Dickens satirized in *Martin Chuzzlewit* under names like *The Sewer*, *The Stabber*, and *The New York Rowdy Journal*. Granted, the language of the press has gotten more sedate in recent times, now that most of the tabloids have folded and reporters have taken to drinking Chardonnay and cosmopolitans. Yet modern newspaper diction still evokes the language of the theatrical melodramas that became popular around the same time as the penny press. It's a tone that disappeared from serious fiction around the 1920s—you don't even hear it much in hard-boiled detective stories nowadays. In fact the only place other than newspapers where you routinely run into verbs like *roil* is in gothic romances and especially pornography, where synonyms for "churn" are always in high demand.

Editors are always deploring the excesses of journalese, but for every embellishment they manage to discourage, three new ones spring up in its place. Along with the spectacular growth of *roil*, for example, the last twenty years have seen sevenfold increases in the use of *ratchet* and *slated*: "As tensions ratchet, new peace talks are slated for next month."

Reporters tell you that they choose words like *roil* and *ratchet* because they were taught in journalism classes that they should try to use action words. Saying that the mayor's decision roiled voters feels more vivid than merely saying that the decision troubled them—it makes it sound as if something has actually taken place since the last edition went to press. The facts may be the same one way or the other, but then journalists know that what sells papers isn't facts but stories—the more dramatic and sanguinary, the better. As a newspaper maxim has it, "If it bleeds, it leads." You can't affect what happened at the city council meeting last night, but you can at least describe it in the same language you'd use to summarize the plot of an Indiana Jones movie—"Embattled Mayor Rips Foes as Deadline Looms." That headline could appear as easily in *The New York Times* as in the *New York Rowdy Journal*; it's just the way the press makes the world sound newsworthy. Melodrama and news were born at the same moment, and they've been talking in the same voice ever since.

[Business Cycles]

For Love or Money

There are few things as dogged as a business writer with a metaphor between his jaws. Here's how *Business Week* described the recent announcement of a merger between two cruise ship lines:

> The path to the altar is strewn with crushed hearts. . . . But no broken engagement between companies has proved quite so stunning as the one that befell Royal Caribbean International. It stood ready to seal a merger with P&O Princess Cruises before a congregation of investors. But then, rival suitor Carnival Cruise Lines swung in. . . . Now, P&O Princess has kissed off Royal Caribbean and is betrothed to Carnival.

That's typical of the way mergers and acquisitions are described nowadays, with a quiverful of words borrowed from the old language of courtship. In fact, the business pages are about the only place this language appears in this day and age. The other day I looked up the first fifty hits for the word *suitor* from a Nexis database of major newspapers. Forty-eight of them involved business deals of one sort or another. One other came from the plot summary of a movie about King Arthur, and the last was from a palace gossip story about the rivals for Princess Di's affections after her separation. *Suitor* isn't a word that pops up a lot on *Sex and the City*.

Or take *woo*. You read about companies wooing investors, politicians wooing voters, and teams wooing fans. But lovers rarely talk about wooing anymore, except in fits of coyness or nostalgia—"You don't suppose you could woo me a little first?"

That language has been in decline for a long time. *Courting* was already on the way out by the late nineteenth century, when people began to feel that the rituals of courtship were impediments to "candor," a favorite word of the romance writers of the period. Anthony Trollope only put *courting* into the mouths of his lower-middle-class and lower-class characters, and within a few years it had become the stuff of rustic comedy. By the beginning of the twentieth century, people were taking up the new slang word *dating*, with its modern egalitarian syntax. Only men could be suitors or go courting, but women could date men as easily as the other way round.

Yet the language still feels right to describe corporate couplings, even if the rest of us have moved on from courtly love to Courtney Love. As that root *court-* reminds us, the vocabulary of courtship has always been drawn from the language of politics and influence, ever since it was cooked up by twelfth-century nobles and troubadours. And the words of courtship have always been charged with double meanings of power and sex. The verb *court* means both to pay amorous attention and to try to gain favor with someone. For that matter, *favor* has the same ambiguity between the meaning "good graces" and its sexual sense—what people used to describe delicately as "the last favor," as in "she granted him the last favor." And until recent times, a "suitor" could be either a lover or a legal petitioner.

Those ambiguities are summed up in the underlying plea of all courtly attentions: Be mine. That's what makes the language a natural fit for the corporate world, the only place left where you can realize your dynastic ambitions by getting someone to change their name to yours. The super-mergers that have built today's corporate giants recall the intricate maneuverings of an age when Catherine of Braganza could arrive in England for her marriage to Charles II with a trousseau bulging with two million crowns and large chunks of India and Morocco.

Even more to the point, the language of courtship has always involved a certain charade of power, as the suitor abases himself in order to gain the upper hand. Samuel Richardson observed that the gallantries always came down to the same message: "I am now, dear Madam, yr humble Servant: Pray be so good as to let me be yr Master." That's a fair paraphrase of the blandishments that companies like Tyco and WorldCom dangled before the companies they were acquiring, and in the end the stockholders wound up in pretty much the same compromised position as Richardson's Clarissa did.

If there's travesty here, it isn't because corporate CEO's are any more devious or rapacious than the courtiers they replaced, but because they're immeasurably more banal. The ardent avowals of courtly love may have been disingenuous, but that's something poetry can be grateful for. Whereas the romance of the modern boardroom is pretty prosaic stuff, in every sense of the term. Imagine what Sidney or Marlowe would have had to come up with if they'd been corporate publicists spinning their companies' takeover bids:

> Come merge with us, and we shall seize
> A thousand win-win synergies.

The Triumph of Capitalism

In the wake of the Enron collapse, Bush administration officials were congratulating themselves for doing nothing to avert the collapse, and indeed were describing it as a vindication of the free market system. The Administration's economic advisor Larry Lindsey called the debacle a "tribute to American capitalism" and Treasury Secretary Paul O'Neill made the point even more fulsomely. "Companies come and go," he said. "Part of the genius of capitalism is people get to make good decisions or bad decisions, and they get to pay the consequence or to enjoy the fruits of their decisions. That's the way the system works."

As even *Business Week* and *Fortune* pointed out, it wasn't exactly the moment for bromides about the genius of capitalism—particularly since the people who had made the bad decisions at Enron weren't the ones who were paying most of the consequences. But Lindsay and O'Neill didn't intend to sound callous. If anything, their remarks showed just how reflexive this sort of rhetoric has become among free-market zealots. It's not just the way they greet each corporate collapse as a triumph of capitalism, but the fact that they mention capitalism at all. Fifteen or twenty years ago, free-market partisans would have been more likely to say, "that's how our free enterprise system works."

Fresh Air Commentary, February 5, 2002

Capitalism has never been a dirty word, exactly. But it has always had a polemical tone, ever since it was given its modern sense by socialist writers in the mid-nineteenth century. The phrase "free enterprise" was invented by economists about a hundred years ago in order to dispel the noxious images that had grown up around *capitalism*—bloated plutocrats, workers bent over their machines, strikebreakers, and the rest. "Free enterprise" wears its ideology on its sleeve. It suggests a connection between political freedom and the right to go about your business without the meddlesome interference of bureaucrats (another word that acquired its pejorative sense around that time). And in place of predatory monopolists like Andrew Carnegie and John D. Rockefeller who were giving capitalism a bad name, "free enterprise" conjures up the plucky young entrepreneurs of the rags-to-riches tales of Horatio Alger.

For most of the twentieth century, "free enterprise" was the homey, chamber-of-commerce name for capitalism. There's a chair of free enterprise at the University of Texas at Austin, a Center for Free Enterprise at the University of South Florida, a Dr Pepper Free Enterprise Institute in Waco, Texas, and a Free Enterprise Leadership Conference held every year by the Jesse Helms center in Wingate, North Carolina. And the word *capitalism* doesn't appear at all in the Web pages of the Horatio Alger Society, a group that honored Kenneth Lay a couple of years ago for, as they put it, "helping young people to . . . value the opportunities presented by America's free enterprise system."

Still, capitalism has always had some defenders who weren't reticent about calling it by its given name, particularly the disciples of Ayn Rand and of libertarian economists like Ludwig von Mises, Frederick Hayek, and Milton Friedman. They tend to be

people who come to the defense of capitalism with something
more like religious zeal.

  You could hear some of that in the profession of faith that
Kenneth Lay made to an interviewer a while ago: "I believe in
God and I believe in free markets," he said, and went on to suggest that Jesus would have agreed with him. Needless to say, that
level of enthusiasm changes the tone of the discussion. When
people extol the virtues of free enterprise, they usually invoke
the rising standard of living and the inventions it spawns. When
they talk about the virtues of capitalism they're more likely to go
on about the moral values of individualism and the freedom to
fail that capitalism provides—the lesson that both O'Neill and
Lindsay were quick to read in the Enron disaster. It's a little scrap
of bombast you can trace directly back to Ayn Rand's turgid phi-
losophizing—the notion that capitalism is never so glorious as
when it's strewing the ground with bodies. (Free-market zealots
also like to use Schumpeter's description of capitalism as "cre-
ative destruction," though they usually neglect to mention
Schumpeter's conclusion that capitalism would wind up by
destroying itself.)

  There was a time when this kind of talk was considered irre-
sponsible by the respectable free-marketeers who were earnestly
promoting the virtues of free enterprise over socialism and the
welfare state. But after the fall of communism and the freewheeling markets of the nineties, *capitalism* is back, and *free enterprise*
has started to sound a little musty. It's gotten to where the word
capitalism was probably as frequent inside the ballrooms at the
World Economic Forum in New York as it was on the signs of the
demonstrators in the street.

  What's odd is that the right's reclamation of the word *capital-*

ism hasn't extended to its cousin *capitalist*. *Forbes* magazine tried to reclaim that word a while ago when it started billing itself as a "capitalist tool," but *capitalist* is still in the closet, at least when used as a job description. People talk about "capitalist societies" or "capitalist economies," and you can describe somebody as a "venture capitalist," which really is just a derivative of "venture capital." But *Forbes* and the *Wall Street Journal* don't ever apply the c-word to people like Bill Gates, Warren Buffett, or Rupert Murdoch. They are investors, entrepreneurs, moguls, or simply businessmen. Reading the business press, you might conclude that America has finally realized the dream of building capitalism without capitalists—that we're free at last from that rapacious class that once held the economy at its mercy. There's no one left to blame; as Secretary O'Neill observed, that's just the way the system works.

A Good Old-Gentlemanly Vice

Supposer que la philosophie veut parler du désir des
richesses, serait trop absurde.

—Proust, *A l'ombre des jeune filles en fleur*, Vol. 1

The other day I looked at a database of major newspapers to see
how often the words *greed* or *greedy* occurred near the words *corporate*, CEO, or *executive*. Not surprisingly, the total is way up for
2002—more than seven times as great as for the same period last
year. And with the threat of a baseball strike looming, the figure
would have been higher still if I'd thrown in the phrases *baseball
players* and *team owners*.

What's more interesting, the word *greed* by itself is a lot more
frequent in all contexts this year than last—up almost 50 percent
since January. It's odd for a common word like that to change its
frequency so rapidly, particularly when it's the name of a basic
human frailty. Whatever people may like to think, it isn't as if the
amount of greed in the world fluctuates the way the number of
school shootings or bankruptcies does.

But the media give a lot more attention to greed at some
times than others, and particularly when the economy is tanking
and everybody's looking for something to blame. When you

chart the frequencies of *greed* and *greedy* in the press, they turn out to be an almost perfect trailing indicator for the stock market—the worse the Dow is doing, the more the media start talking about greediness. The words declined steadily between 1994 and 2000, and then they shot up again, until they returned to a near-record level this summer, when all the market indexes were at five-year lows. In the press, the summers of greed seem always to follow the winters of our discontent.

It's striking that the press talks about greed as much as it does. In newspapers, the word is 50 percent more common than *envy*. That's very different from what you'd find if you followed ordinary people around with a tape recorder. Greed seems to be a purely public dereliction—it isn't something we talk about much in daily life. In my household we sometimes throw the adjective *greedy* around, but only in a jocular way, and more often in reference to pizza than to money—"Don't get greedy! You already had two slices." But getting greedy is just a momentary lapse, not a moral condition. And *greed* isn't the word that comes to mind when I think about the people I know who seem to take an excessive interest in money and material possessions. I might question their values, but I don't think of their problem as a sin—it's more in the line of a having disorder.

Maybe this is just a matter of perspective. However you define it, greed always comes down to wanting more than your fair share. And at the scale of everyday life, it's easier to see what counts as more than a fair share of a pizza than more than a fair share of money. In fact I'll bet most people would have a hard time thinking of themselves as greedy under any circumstances, given that the notion of "a fair share" is wonderfully elastic.

If it didn't have its public career to sustain it, *greed* would probably sound as quaint and biblical as words like *sloth* and *wrath* and *gluttony* do. Or for that matter *lust*, another word that most people nowadays use only in a jocular way—"I was really lusting after those shoes." But the fact that we don't think about greed in everyday settings is exactly what makes it a useful notion to keep around in public life—it's so remote that we can all denounce it with a clear conscience. People tend to talk about greed as a collective pathology rather than an individual vice. In the press, I'm always running into references to corporate greed and investor greed, to greedy developers and greedy oil companies. But writers rarely use *greed* and *greedy* to describe particular people, apart from rapacious movie villains and a couple of poster-child miscreants who have actually been caught dead to rights. Even then, there's a striking discrepancy: Enron is twenty-five times more likely to be described with *greed* or *greedy* than Kenneth Lay is.

But the remoteness of greed from our private life doesn't simply make it easy to condemn, it makes it easy to defend. That's what explains the success of the slogan "greed is good." That phrase was originally supposed to evoke the audience's repugnance when Michael Douglas uttered it in the movie *Wall Street*, taking it in turn from an actual remark of the financier Ivan Boesky. But the champions of the market system have adopted it as a defiant way of praising untrammeled acquisitiveness as the source of economic growth and all the good things it brings with it.

There's nothing new about this notion—two hundred years ago, David Hume called avarice "the spur of industry." It's hard to imagine anyone fashioning a similar catchphrase for the other deadly sins: "Gluttony is groovy"; "Sloth is splendid." But then greed is a more conveniently removed vice than the others—you can praise it in the abstract without expecting that anybody is actually going to own up to it. Jack Welch isn't about to claim in his autobiography that he owes his success to his overweening greed, nor is the guy in the TV repair shop going to crow about the social benefits of greed when he's explaining why he's charging you seventy-five bucks to make an estimate. However people try to redeem it, there's no sin that's privately more shameful and unlovable than greed, what the poet Matthew Green described as "the sphincter of the heart."

The Vision Thing

There was a picturesque footnote to the Enron affair in the names that the company picked for those offshore corporations that it used to hide its losses, which were drawn from action adventure films like *Braveheart, Jurassic Park,* and above all the *Star Wars* movies, which contributed names like Jedi Capital, Obi–1 Holdings, and Kenobe, Inc. In retrospect, those names were clearly a symptom of the space-cadet mentality of the company's top management. But the fondness for *Star Wars* imagery isn't restricted to one rogue outfit in Houston. George Lucas has probably had more influence on the language of corporate America than any other single individual, with Vince Lombardi and Fritz Perls running neck-and-neck for second.

This has less to do with Lucas's cinematic imagination than with a problem that has haunted corporate America ever since the early twentieth century, when large corporations definitively replaced the family firm as the dominant economic force. How do you motivate employees to feel a sense of loyalty or commitment to an abstract entity like a corporation? In the words of Peter Drucker, the first and the only great theorist that the corporation has ever had: "An engineer will not be motivated to make a shareholder rich."

Fresh Air Commentary, March 25, 2002

That problem became more urgent about twenty years ago, as corporations started to bail out on the traditional promise of lifetime employment, and as the salary gap between employees and top managers began to swell. That's when corporations and consultants started talking about creating "high-performance corporate cultures." The term was meant to suggest that purely symbolic rewards and motivations could move employees to feel a loyalty and esprit de corps that went beyond anything that was justified by material considerations alone. Consultants claimed that a company with a strong corporate culture could gain an hour of productive daily work from every employee.

What made the new conception of "culture" different from old-fashioned "morale" is the way corporations tried to shape it. The fashioning of corporate culture is largely—and often, almost exclusively—a matter of linguistic engineering, as managers try to invest the corporation with the features that inspire loyalty in other walks of life. Writing just after World War II, when the country had come together in a swell of patriotic spirit, Drucker suggested that corporations ought to think of themselves as miniature polities, the representative institutions of society. But modern corporations haven't found the language of civic engagement a very inspiring model. It's not stirring enough, for one thing, and it focuses too much on individualism and democratic consensus. However you package it, it's hard to make a corporation look like anything but an oligarchy.

At first blush, the military would seem to be a better model. But modern military language sounds more corporate than martial nowadays, with its predilection for acronyms and euphemisms like "collateral damage." And not even a bank or insurance company would venture to refer to its employees as "assets."

What corporations really wanted their employees to feel like was the combatants in medieval romances, setting out on quests in the face of implacable, inhuman enemies and driven by a spiritual sense of mission. That's what the space operas made their stock-in-trade—Sir Gawain on the holodeck. So it's no accident that shortly after movies like *Star Wars, Star Trek,* and *Mad Max* began to appear, corporations started to loot their language. Salespeople became "road warriors" and the people who shepherd new products and initiatives through development were called "champions." Above all, that was when corporations started to come up with "vision statements" and "mission statements." Those were posted on walls or Web sites and printed on wallet-sized cards that employees were expected to carry on their persons at all times, like the sacramental badges called scapulars that the members of monastic fraternities wear under their clothing.

In the end, these vision statements almost always come down to the same bromides and generalities that have been around for years under the headings of goals and mottoes. "Our vision is to seek long-term growth by providing innovative, high-quality products that create significant value for our customers." That's an unimpeachable objective, whether you're selling eyeglasses or heavy equipment. But thirty years ago, no one would have thought to describe it as a vision, a word that used to be reserved for people like Saint Teresa of Avila.

Whatever you tell them, of course, most corporate employees aren't at risk of confusing themselves with Luke Skywalker. In fact the chief effect of all that *Star Wars* talk about missions and visions has been to exacerbate employees' sense of disaffection, all the more because it seems to devalue the everyday dedi-

cation that most people actually bring to their jobs. In private life
it's enough to have goals and hopes, but when you arrive at the
workplace now your eyes are expected to be glistening with some
nobler sense of purpose. I recall what a friend told me about having to compose a vision statement for his job: "It isn't enough
that I give them my body—now they want me to kiss them on
the mouth."

But then the real audience for this language isn't so much the
employees it's addressed to as the executives who commission it.
In an age when successful CEO's are routinely treated as media
stars, top managers no longer model themselves after traditional
corporate sages like Alfred Sloan or Thomas Watson. They'd
rather think of themselves in the image of General Patton or
Captain Kirk, leading their troops into battle as they trail a cloud
of rousing metaphors behind them. However dreary or dull your
friends may find you, it isn't hard to think of yourself as a charis-
matic leader when you've got a communications department
churning out yards of fulsome panegyric. Not long ago I saw a
Xerox Corporation press release that said, "The senior team . . .
spontaneously erupted into sustained applause and stood as a
sign of respect to their new leader"—language that would have
made even a Stalinist apparatchik blush.

In the end, though, the real victims of this sort of talk aren't
the cynical employees who shine it on but the trusting ones who
buy into the story and load up their 401K's with the company's
stock. And then when the Death Star explodes, the Force is
nowhere to be found.

Initiating Mission-Critical Jargon Reduction

Asking a business consulting firm to repair the damage business itself has done to the English language may feel a bit like entrusting the school nutrition program to Taco Bell. Nonetheless, since last month almost 100,000 people have downloaded Bullfighter, a free program from Deloitte Consulting that plugs into Microsoft Word and PowerPoint and flags jargon like *best of breed* and *synergies* and proposes ordinary English alternatives.

Over the past twenty years, business has replaced the bureaucracy in the public mind as the chief perpetrator of doublespeak. On the Web, references to corporate or business jargon outnumber references to bureaucratic or government jargon by three to one. It's a remarkable shift in attitudes, particularly since government hasn't exactly been sleeping on the job.

True, complaints about the language of business aren't new. Critics have long griped about the use of *contact* as a verb. Back in 1931, a Western Union vice president called the verb "a hideous vulgarism" and banned it from company documents, and H. L. Mencken described it in 1936 as one of the "counter words" of "the heyday of Babbittry." (The condemnation is repeated in the latest edition of Strunk and White's *The Elements of Style*, which is

The New York Times Week in Review, August 3, 2003

apparently still holding out for "write, phone, fax, wire, e-mail or click on us.") And mid–twentieth-century businessmen were ridiculed for inventions like *performancewise* and *depreciationwise*—a vogue promoted by *Fortune* magazine, which Archibald MacLeish once described as "understaffed good-writer-wise."

Still, it's hard to get over the impression that where there's smoke, there's downsizing. Business jargon may not be new, but it's more visible and more pervasive in corporate life than it used to be.

Strategists and consultants bandy clichés like *coopetition*, *low-hanging fruit*, and *mission-critical*, which repackage old concepts in shiny new shrinkwrap. Human resources departments (Mencken would have loved that name) have appropriated the language of the human potential movement to smooth the edges of hierarchy and conflict—"Let's revisit that issue to align our end-state visions." Naming consultants churn out high-tech portmanteau names, with an eye to how they will play on Wall Street rather than on the factory floor.

And then there's the stiff-gaited swagger of managerial slang. I recall a line from a memo I received on the day I started work at a corporate research lab: "Cascade this to your people and see what the push-back is." If that sentence were a person, it would walk like George W. Bush.

It's tempting to see all this as the sign of an increase in managerial pretension and fatuity. That's the view according to Dilbert, which depicts the modern office as something like the England of Walter Scott's Ivanhoe, where hard-working English-speaking serfs are oppressed by supercilious overlords who speak a foreign tongue. That picture appeals not just to the grunts in the cube-farms, but to their corporate superiors, who find Dilbert's dimwitted boss as risible as everybody else does.

In fact Dilbert's creator, Scott Adams, has made a lucrative sideline out of helping management get its message across. In his consulting capacity, Dilbert has enabled Honda of America to "develop the key message [that] quality is a core value" and helped Xerox to invest employees with the "sense of ownership" that comes from an "empowering work environment."

That's the curious thing about corporate jargon—everyone deplores it, but nobody can resist it. The Deloitte division that developed BullFighter promises "thought-leading research" that "empowers global enterprises." A promotional brochure from a large British law firm offers its clients "tax compliance advice which is effective, clear and jargon-free," and continues: "Our approach is proactive. We also believe that tax rules can play a positive role in incentivizing investors."

Reading that, you're struck less by its pretension than by its ingenuousness—it reminds you of Molière's M. Jordain, who was astonished to learn he had been speaking prose all his life. But blaming the proliferation of business cant on an increase in phoniness is like blaming the recent corporate scandals on a sudden uptick in greed. Both are the outgrowths of the changing nature of the corporation itself. If there's an invisible hand that moves the market, there sometimes seems to be an invisible mouth that speaks for it.

Consultants like to talk about "building high-performance corporate cultures," but as with a lot of the things we distinguish as cultures nowadays, the differences between corporations are actually pretty superficial. If they weren't, people wouldn't all be using the same jargon and papering their cubicle walls with the same comic strips, nor would top managers find it so easy to move from soft-drink companies to computer firms. But America does have *a* culture of the corporation, and it is increasingly detached from the values that are touchstones in our personal dealings. Few people nowadays perceive the historical connection between *private sector* and *private life*.

The corporation was created as a legal fiction to reduce personal responsibility. The new language merely acknowledges that function. Reducing your work force to cut costs doesn't carry the same moral stigma as dismissing an old family retainer. It's understandable that managers would want to find other words for the process—it's nothing personal, after all.

Yet some companies do manage to talk more plainly than others—Deloitte points to Home Depot and Apple Computer—and in fact the evidence suggests that that's a good indicator of a company's financial well-being.

Not that curbing jargon is likely to do much for a company's bottom line all by itself. But it can't do any harm to call people on the buzzwords they use. It's like requiring gang members to leave their colors at home and wear blazers and ties to school—it may not subdue their obstreperous natures, but it makes those cocky poses a little harder to strike.

Farewell to the Alero

Detroit's recent interest in nostalgia isn't limited to retro designs like the Plymouth Prowler and the Chrysler PT Cruiser—it carries over to naming, as well. Two years ago General Motors successfully revived the Impala name for its full-size Chevrolets, and last month at the Detroit Auto Show the company debuted a new concept convertible that bears the name of the old Chevy Bel Air.

But it's one thing to revive a name and another to revive the context that gave it its meaning. As the linguist Mark Aronoff has observed, there has probably been no purer example of semiotic manipulation than the wheel of brands that the Big Three automakers devised in the 1950s and 1960s. Back then, every American make of car had several distinct models for each of its lines, full-sized, mid-sized, and compact. In 1958, there were three full-sized Chevrolet models, the deluxe Bel Air, the standard Biscayne, and the economy Delray. The Impala was introduced in that year as a special edition of the Bel Air. Then the next year the Impala became a separate model of its own, and the other models were demoted: the Bel Air became the standard model, the Biscayne became the new economy model, and the old economy Delray was dropped.

Fresh Air Commentary, February 14, 2002

The same process was repeated a few years later when Chevy introduced a new deluxe model called the Caprice and demoted the Impala and Bel Air a notch, eliminating the Biscayne name at the bottom. The cycle was the same at Chrysler and Ford. The Fairlane, the Galaxie, the LTD—each of them started out as a limited edition deluxe model, then worked its way gradually down the chain to the economy slot.

While it lasted, it was the most elaborate and successful experiment ever undertaken in the semantic manipulation of demand. Every few years a new name was introduced, fastened to a rare and desirable object, and then over time the cars it was attached to were made cheaper and more accessible, to the point where anyone could have one. It was as close to a traffic in pure names as any marketer has ever been able to sustain. In 1978, Chevy discontinued selling its Vega compacts, which had been plagued by highly publicized engine defects, but continued selling some of the Vega cars under the Monza line.

It was also probably the most wasteful marketing strategy ever devised. Companies deliberately degraded their established brand names just to increase the demand for new ones, like a builder who lets an apartment complex go to seed so that tenants will want to move into the one he's putting up next door.

What was remarkable was that consumers were willing to buy into the illusions that the system rested on. In fact there was virtually no difference between the models, apart from the options and trim. The main feature that distinguished the deluxe Chevy models from the standard and economy models was that they had three little round tail lights on each side, rather than two, in the same way Buick distinguished its upmarket models by putting an extra porthole on its front fenders. Those were features that the manufacturers tended to maintain even when the rest of the design was radically changed to preserve the illusion that the Bel Air or the Impala was "the same car" from one year to the next.

But the great wheel of model names could only keep turning so long as the car companies could assume that consumers had nowhere else to go—that people would be willing to spend their entire lives climbing the ladder of GM brands even as the company kept throwing more grease on the rungs. By the mid-1970s, consumers were becoming less willing to replace their cars every few years just so they could own the new model, partly because new car prices were rising much more rapidly than the average family income, and partly because the Japanese and Europeans were grabbing large parts of the U.S. market with brand names that kept their luster over the long haul. By the eighties American carmakers were offering only one model per line.

All of that led to changes in the kinds of names that manufacturers were putting on their models. The car names of the '50s and '60s were based on a few unimaginative patterns—most were taken from the names of exotic destinations, like the Monte Carlo and the Seville; from animals, like the Mustang and Impala; or from vaguely superlative words, like the Regal and the Invicta. But the associations of those names weren't what mattered— their real connotations came from their place in the constellation of brands, and shifted as they were rotated from deluxe to standard to economy.

Only when the system broke down in the late 1970s did car marketers take to using fanciful names, in the fond hope that they could evoke the car's character all by themselves. That's when the companies began appropriating random English words or hatching jumbles of nonsense syllables. Inevitably, car names started to sound like the names of other products. A Monte Carlo or Mustang could only be a car. But Prodigy, Protégé, Prizm, Precis, Prius—those could as easily be digital cameras or office productivity software (actually, Prius sounds more like a treatment for erectile dysfunction). And other names sounded like they should be attached to china patterns or cosmetics lines. Korando, Elantra, Vitara, Nubira—they're words out of some lingua branda of the far future, what we'll all speak when the last common noun has been trademarked.

Among the Big Three, names like these started to become anxious incantations, as if the carmakers believed the right string of syllables could somehow conjure a market niche out of nowhere. Long before General Motors announced this year that it was phasing out the Oldsmobile brand, you could tell the division was in trouble just from the desperation of its model names in the late '90s: Alero, Achieva, Bravada, Ciera. It was a sad dotage for the brand that gave us classic model names like the Rocket 88, the Futuramic 98, the Starfire, and the Toronado. GM may some day bring back the names of some of those vintage Oldsmobiles, particularly if the nostalgia vogue continues. But it's safe to say we've heard the last of Alero.

100 Percent Solutions

I got a mail-order catalog the other day from a company that specializes in various home and health-care products. At least they used to call them products, but now that word has been entirely eliminated from their catalog in favor of *solutions*. You can find seat cushions in the section on "stress relief solutions," bathrobes in "spa care solutions," and support bras in "intimate apparel solutions."

The solutions game began in the early 1980s, when companies like IBM started using the word to describe the packages of hardware, software, and services they were selling to corporate customers. In a sense it's just a new way of pitching your offerings as answers to customers' needs and anxieties, in the time-honored tradition of ring-around-the-collar and the heartbreak of psoriasis. Except that *solutions* makes its point in a proactive way. Time was, when people said, "I've got a solution for you" you could assume that somebody had mentioned a problem somewhere along the line. Now the two have come unhitched—solutions aren't solutions *for* anything anymore. When you do a search on "solutions" at the Web site of Compaq or Apple Computer, you find that it's anywhere from two to three times as frequent as "problems." Business people don't like to hear someone talk about "problems"—the P-word. It seems to betray a negative mindset—if there are difficulties you absolutely have to mention, you try to find another name for them. As in "We had a number of challenges this quarter," or "There are several known issues installing the beta release of the printer driver."

By now there are hundreds of firms that have incorporated *solutions* into their company names, and by no means all of them are high-tech. There's the beachwear maker Sun Solutions, which is not to be confused with Solar Solutions, which sells propane ranges and composting toilets. Ondeo Solutions builds sewage-treatment facilities. And then there's Bright Horizons Family Solutions, an outfit that manages corporate daycare centers, whose portfolio presumably includes story-hour solutions and snack solutions, not to mention nap solutions for clients with crankiness issues.

It's hard to think of a company that *couldn't* say it was in the solutions business now. ("Smuckers, your toast-coating solutions provider.") In fact, one reason why so many companies are sticking *solutions* into their names is that they don't have to let on as to what they're actually selling, particularly if they're still in the slightly embarrassing business of making Things. Things have low margins and high capital costs. They're expensive to ship, they lead to liability lawsuits, they get you in trouble with the EPA. If you make them domestically you have to deal with unions. If you make them overseas, people get on your back for running sweatshops.

It's no wonder the manufacturing sector is a diminishing part of the American economy. In 1950, material goods made up more than half the Gross Domestic Product; now they account for less than a quarter of it. And companies that aren't in a position to stop making Things altogether can at least re-label them as solutions. It suggests that their products are just an ancillary sideline of their real business, like the terrycloth slippers they throw in when you go for a massage.

That's the beauty of *solutions*—companies don't have to tip their hands. It's a perfect complement for those empty corporate names that marketing consultants paste together out of strings of chopped-up syllables. Take the Ohio outfit called Omnova Solutions. What line of work would you say they're in—client-server applications? healthcare benefits administration? Actually it's fabric transfers and decorative wall coverings, but the others are just as plausible. These aren't like those old-fashioned corporate names that were designed to conjure up an image of a real product made by a real company. You feel sorry for the members of a softball team who have to take the field with "Omnova Solutions" written on their uniforms.

Names like these are attempts to create pure brands, free signifiers that float in the ether ready to light on anything that somebody's willing to pay for. That's what the new economy comes down to, in the end—just one big intersection with people at every corner holding signs that say, "Will solve for cash."

[Tech Talk]

As Google Goes, So Goes the Nation

You don't get to be a verb unless you're doing something right. Do a Google search on "ford," for example, and the first batch of results includes the pages for the Ford Motor Company, the Ford Foundation, the Betty Ford Center, Harrison Ford, and Gerald R. Ford—all good guesses at what a user would be looking for, particularly considering that Google estimates its index holds more than 16 million pages including the word.

Google now conducts 55 percent of all searches on the World Wide Web. People have come to trust the service to act as a digital bloodhound—give it a search term to sniff, and it disappears into the cyber wilderness, returning a fraction of a second later with the site you were looking for in its mouth.

The importance attached to a high Google ranking has led people to try to game the system, arranging to trade links with other high-volume sites or paying other sites to link to them. Commercial sites use those techniques to try to get more traffic, and pranksters and activists have used similar methods to engage in "googlebombing"—a way of hijacking a search term, so that the first result of a search on, say, "Joe's Garage" will be a page that derogates the firm.

The New York Times Week in Review, May 18, 2003

But a high Google ranking can also have a lot of clout in the marketplace of ideas. It seems to confer ownership on a particular word or phrase—deciding, in effect, who gets to define it. It's easy to read these results as reflecting the consensus of an extended Internet community, with the power to shape opinion and events. As James F. Moore, a fellow at the Berkman Center for Internet and Society at Harvard Law School, wrote in an article on his blog, the Internet has become a "shared collective mind" that is coming to figure as a "second superpower."

Sometimes, though, the deliberations of the collective mind seem to come up short. Take Moore's use of "second superpower" to refer to the Internet community. Not long ago, an article on the British technology site The Register accused Moore of "googlewashing" that expression—in effect, hijacking the expression and giving it a new meaning.

The phrase had actually originated in a February 17 article by Patrick E. Tyler in *The New York Times* that referred to the United States and world public opinion as the "two superpowers on the planet." Shortly after that, "second superpower" was adopted by organizations like Greenpeace and was used by Kofi Annan, the United Nations secretary-general, to refer to antiwar opinion. But Moore's article using the phrase to refer to the collective mind of the Internet was linked to by a number of bloggers sympathetic to his ideas, and quickly became the first hit returned when someone searches Google for "second superpower."

There was nothing underhanded in Moore's ability to co-opt ownership of the phrase in the rankings; it follows from the way Google works. Google's algorithms rank results both by looking at how prominently the search terms figure in the pages that include them and by taking advantage of what Google calls "the uniquely democratic nature of the Web" to estimate the popularity of a site. It gives a higher rank to pages that are linked to by a number of other pages, particularly if the referring pages themselves are frequently linked to. (The other major search engines have adopted similar techniques.)

When you search for a common item like *ford* or *baseball*, the engines naturally give the highest rankings to major sites that are linked to by hundreds or thousands of other pages. But when searches are more specific—whether for "second superpower" or "Sinatra arrangers"—the rankings will mirror the interests of the groups that aggregate around particular topics: the bloggers, experts, activists, hobbyists, or, every so often, the crackpots.

Not long ago a German friend of mine went to Google for help in refuting a colleague who maintained that American authorities engineered the attacks of September 11, 2001, citing as evidence, among other things, the delay in sending American fighter jets aloft that morning. My friend did searches on a number of obvious strings, like "9/11 scramble jets intercept." But almost all the pages that came up were the work of conspiracy theorists, with titles like "Guilty for 9–11: Bush, Rumsfeld, Myers" and "Pentagon surveillance videos—where are the missing frames?" As my friend put it, "To judge from the Google results, there's plenty of evidence for a conspiracy and little to the contrary."

That's the sort of result that often leads people to complain that the Web is full of junk or that the search engines aren't working as they should. From the standpoint of the search engines, however, this is all as it should be. The beauty of the Web, after all, is that it enables us to draw on the expertise of people who take a particular interest in a topic and are willing to take the trouble to set down what they think about it. In that sense, the Web is a tool that enables people who have a life to benefit from the efforts of those who don't.

Given the "uniquely democratic" nature of the Web, it shouldn't be surprising that the votes reported by the search engines have many of the deficiencies of plebiscites in the democracies on the other side of the screen. On topics of general interest, the rankings tend to favor the major sites and marginalize the smaller or newer ones; here, as elsewhere, money and power talk.

When it comes to more specialized topics, the rankings sometimes give disproportionate weight to opinions of the activists and enthusiasts that can be at odds with the views of the larger public. It's as if the United Nations General Assembly made all its decisions by referring the question to whichever nation cares most about the issue: The Swiss get to rule on watchmaking, the Japanese on whaling.

The outcomes of Google's popularity contests can be useful to know, but it's a mistake to believe they reflect the consensus of the "Internet community," whatever that might be, or to think of the Web as a single vast colloquy—the picture that's implicit in all the talk of the Internet as a "digital commons" or "collective mind." Seen from a Google's eye view, in fact, the Web is less like a piazza than a souk—a jumble of separate spaces, each with its own isolated chatter. The search engines cruise the alleyways to listen in on all of these conversations, locate the people who are talking about the subject we're interested in, and tell us which of them has earned the most nods from the other confabulators in the room. But just because someone is regarded as a savant in the barbershop doesn't mean he'll pass for wise with the people in the other stalls.

I Have Seen the Future, and It Blogs

The Diary of a Nobody is a curious comic classic. It was published in 1892 by George and Weedon Grossmith, two well-known Victorian music-hall performers, adapted from a series of pieces they had written in *Punch*. It purported to be the diary of a clerk named Mr. Charles Pooter, who lives in the drab London suburb of Holloway. Mr. Pooter is a bumbling, self-important, and slightly pathetic character who dutifully records his daily encounters with tradesmen, neighbors, and co-workers. You can get a sense of the tone from the chapter descriptions: "A conversation with Mr. Merton on society. Tradesmen still troubling. I make a good joke, but Gowing and Cummings are unnecessarily offended. I paint the bath red, with unexpected result." That density of humdrum detail is what fixes Mr. Pooter's diary in its particular historical moment, and it's also why people are still reading it more than a hundred years later.

If the Grossmiths were living today, I feel sure they would have written Mr. Pooter's chronicle as a blog. For those who still associate that syllable with the French word for "joke," I should explain that *blog* is short for weblog. Weblogs began their lives as a cross between news digests and clipping services—regularly

updated sites where someone put up links to other sites of interest, often with comments and personal asides. Most of the early
blogs were dedicated to specialized interests like programming,
motorcycles, or martial arts, and lately there have been a number
of blogs coming from journalists and political commentators.

But the great boom in blogging came from people who put
up personal journals at their home pages, updating them daily.
Bloggers linked to other bloggers. Blogrings formed, then blog
registries, blog hosting sites, and metablogs. There are blog divas,
who receive thousands of hits a day, and the wannabes called blog
whores, who inveigle other bloggers to link to their pages. There
are racy blogs and philosophical blogs and depressive blogs—there
are quite a number of depressive blogs. There are blog groupies
and blog stalkers. And there are quarterly blog awards.

To get a sense of the blog world, you're best off following
links aimlessly, or clicking on the "random blog" link at a hosting
site like OpenPages. A sixty-year-old poet in Somerset ruminates
on Robert Frost and gives his recipe for corned beef hash. A nine-
teen-year-old boy frets over having only ten months left as a
teenager. A Sacramento lawyer named Elizabeth dilates divert-
ingly on the differences among "Beth," "Betsy," and "Betty."

Like most of the phenomena of the Web, blogging is con-
nected to a lot of things that have been going on on the other
side of the screen—the journaling that has been part of the self-
help movement, reality TV, the mimeographed Christmas letters
that people send out to friends and family. For that matter, there's
nothing new about publishing a daily journal—that's a tradition
that stretches from Defoe and Boswell to Edmund Wilson and
Anais Nin. But journal publishing has never been a democratic
option before, or something that was carried out with so much

collaboration and corroboration. Readers write in with encouragement for an AIDS-infected singer-composer in Los Angeles. A woman in San Francisco puts up a webcam and asks readers if they think she ought to streak her hair. A college freshman posts a blog recounting his painfully inept day-to-day quest to find a girlfriend, as readers offer him dating tips.

People often talk about "blog communities," but "community" is too vague to have much meaning here. Blogs aren't written for friends and family—in fact a lot of the sites warn off anyone who knows the writer from reading further. But they aren't really public records, either, at least not in the sense that the word has in a phrase like "the reading public." It's more a question of someone writing a journal *in* public—it's not addressed to everybody so much as to god-knows-who.

What's most compelling about the blogs is their incessant dailyness. The other day I was looking at an entry in the blog of a young woman from Boston. She described a trip to Baltimore that she had made with her boyfriend, in numbing, mile-by-mile detail, and accompanied it with photographs of the Dunkin' Donuts where they had breakfast, the flag they saw on the George Washington Bridge, and the copy of *Cosmopolitan* she was reading on the road. When I mentioned that entry to my friend Lisa, who keeps a blog of her own, she said, "That's what we call oversharing."

I could see her point, but the entry had a certain Pooterish fascination, too. There's something very familiar about that accretion of diurnal detail. It's what the novel was trying to achieve when eighteenth-century writers cobbled it together out of subliterary genres like personal letters, journals, and newspapers, with the idea of reproducing the inner and outer experience that makes up daily life. If ever any literary genre that interesting should emerge from the intimate anonymity of cyberspace, it will probably grow out of offhand forms like the blog, not the "migration" of the novel to digital form.

But that doesn't really matter, as long as people are having fun. And in the meantime, we can visit the blogs for glimpses of other lives, in all their humdrum glory. Or if we're looking for an older sort of collaborative journal, we can call up George and Weedon Grossmith's *Diary of a Nobody*. It's on the Web, too.

Prefixed Out

I did a piece on blogs a couple of months ago. After it ran I got an e-mail from someone who objected to my use of the word, particularly using it to describe the records that people post on the Web of their daily thoughts and doings. I should have called them "e-journals," she said. I could see her point, but *blog* is a syllable whose time has come. Who can resist that paleolithic pizzazz? It's the tone you hear in a lot of programmer jargon, in words like *kluge, munge,* and *scrog.* That's how insiders demystify the technology—it sets them apart from the digital parvenus who lade their speech with technical-sounding language. When we use *blog,* it's as if to say we're all geeks now.

Anyway, there's something a little *vieux jeu* about the whole business of naming online phenomena by tacking a qualifier onto the name of some predigital category. First there was *cyber-,* which had its efflorescence in the first half of the '90s. Those were the salad days of cyberspace—not the noirish locale that William Gibson had in mind when he coined the word, but more like something out of C. S. Lewis, an enchanted kingdom on the other side of the screen where everything had an ethereal cyber-counterpart: cybercrime and cyberpolice; cyberpoetry and cybernovels; cyberpets and cyberhippies. *Cyber-* connoted a place that was freed from the trammels of materiality and distance, where people would slip on new identities as easily as they changed their shirts. You think of the caption on a widely reprinted cartoon that Peter Steiner did in *The New Yorker* back in 1993: "On the Internet, nobody knows you're a dog."

By the mid-1990s, though, the *cyber-* talk was sounding awfully naïve. The net was becoming crowded, noisy, and above all lucrative. And it was turning out to be anything but anonymous—it was more like, "On the Internet, everybody knows what brand of dog food you buy." After 1996, the word *cyberspace* became less frequent in the press. The gold rush was on, and people migrated to the new prefix *e-*, which seemed to be short for Eldorado.

The *e-* prefix had a promising beginning—in 1998 the American Dialect Society voted it the new word that was most likely to succeed. Like a lot of predictions about the Internet that people were making back then, that one would turn out to be excessively optimistic. When you track the frequency of *e-* in the press, in fact, its fortunes almost exactly parallel the NASDAQ index—by 2001, it was 60 percent off its peak. And *e-* isn't likely to make a comeback even when the tech sector reemerges, no more than most of the companies whose names began with it. It will stick around in *e-commerce* and of course *e-mail*, the way *cyber-* is still around in a few words like *cybersex*—maybe the last thing in digital life that has a touch of intrigue to it. But we've left off thinking of the online world as a remote or separate place. For the time being, at least, the new economy is going to be just a neighborhood of the old—and one with a higher vacancy rate, at that.

Anyway, most of those distinctions are unnecessary. Why the

prefix on *cyberessay* and *cyberpoetry*—are essays and poetry really transformed once you no longer have to send them to the printer? Ditto *e-statements* and *e-bills*, not to mention all the increasingly desperate names that were coined with *i-* and *k-*, as companies started to switch prefixes as rapidly as business plans. For that matter, what's the point of talking about a "virtual bait-shop," so long as the crawlers are real?

Of course a lot of the things that have emerged online are genuinely novel, but then why strain to find their offline counterparts? That's the beauty of *blog*. You could call these things virtual journals, e-clipping services, or cyber-Christmas-letters. But why can't they just be unique in all their bloggy essence?

We go through this every time a new technology emerges. It took a while before people could stop talking about horseless carriages, electric iceboxes, and electronic brains, but in the end those hybrid names always wind up sounding quaint, and so will all those compounds with *cyber-*, *e-*, *virtual*, and the rest. If we were smart, we'd drag them all to the trash icon of history right now. But that isn't likely to happen. They'll end their days attached to useless computer accessories and get-rich-quick schemes, the same way the suffix *-omatic* migrated from the names of all those proud postwar Fords and Buicks to the tacky gadgets they sell on late-night TV.

The Icebox Goeth

This was one of those upstairs-downstairs exchanges we have in our house when my twelve-year-old daughter Sophie is getting breakfast. "Dad, where's the maple syrup?" I yell back, "I put it in the icebox." A pause, then Sophie yells back, "Dad, it's not there." And I answer, "Yes it is, on the top shelf, next to the milk." "Oh," she says, "you mean down there. I thought you said it was in the *ice box*, on the top."

I apologized to her. It wasn't Sophie's fault that her dad is behind the curve in the nomenclature of domestic life. Actually, what's curious is that I or anybody should still be saying *icebox*. That fixture started to disappear from American kitchens in the 1920s, when electric and gas-powered refrigerators first became available for home use. The new machines went by names like Coolerator, Frigerator, Coldak, and most famously Frigidaire, but at the time most people just referred to them as gas or electric ice boxes. A joke in *Life* magazine in 1925 poked fun at the vogue for newfangled household appliances: A bride at a telephone says, "Oh, John, do come home, I've mixed the plugs some way. The radio is all covered with frost and the electric ice box is singing *Way Out West in Kansas*." And *icebox* has persisted since then, even though the last iceman hung up his tongs long ago.

Fresh Air Commentary, January 24, 2002

That's usually the way things work when a new technology or new way of doing things appears—we tend to keep calling it by the name of what it replaces, even long after it's appropriate. We still refer to the luggage compartments at the back of our cars as trunks—not even Sophie objects to that one. And we're still talking about dialing telephones, even though the old sort of dial has become such a rarity that we've had to invent a new description for it, the "rotary dial."

Rotary dial is what some people call a retronym, a term that expresses a distinction that didn't used to be necessary. *Analogue watch* is a retronym, and so are *natural turf* and *Mainland China*. You can get a good sense of the pace of change over the past century just by looking at the retronyms we've accumulated. New technologies have forced us to come up with terms like *steam locomotive, silent movie, manual transmission, AM radio, day baseball, conventional oven,* and *acoustic guitar*. Cultural changes created retronyms like *physical therapy, heterosexual marriage,* and *men's wrestling*. And now we've had to introduce another set of terms to distinguish things in the material world from their virtual counterparts—*surface mail, face-to-face conference, brick-and-mortar retailer,* and—God save us all—*paper book*.

You could think of this torrent of retronyms as a reflection of the pliable metaphysics of modern life. Nowadays everything can be estranged from its essence: We can make watches without hands, beer without alcohol, grapes without seeds, ovens without heat, and babies without sex. But the phenomenon also has a lot to do with simple linguistic laziness. We start by calling a microwave an oven because it's too much trouble to come up with a new name, then later we have to go back and find a modifier like "conventional" to distinguish the old sort of ovens.

And yet sometimes we're curiously reluctant to let an old

word do new tricks. We may talk about "electronic mail," for example, but we don't describe the online messages we receive as "electronic letters," maybe out of nostalgia for the smell of ink and paper. We're reluctant to stretch *broadcast* to cover the cable transmission of television programs. And while we allow that photos can be digital, we still reserve the phrase "home movies" for images recorded on film—otherwise they're videos.

Why do we refuse to extend some names to new categories while readily extending others? Is it out of a sense that the new thing is essentially different from the old one? Is it nostalgia? Marketing? Or just linguistic inconsistency? Those sound like the kinds of questions my friends and I used to idle our evenings away with back when we were in graduate school. But sometimes a lot hangs in the balance.

Take the word *copy*. When we say that a computer makes a copy of a file to your hard disk, are we talking about the same thing as the copy that we make when we take a book to the Xerox machine? If they're the same, then the major publishers have a lot more power in the digital age than they had in the age of print. Time Warner or Bertelsmann can't stop you from lending a hard copy of a magazine article to a friend, but they can stop you from sending it around as an e-mail attachment, since you can't do that without making an electronic copy of the document. But some legal scholars argue that a digital copy isn't at all the same kind of thing as a physical copy, no more than my new Amana is the same kind of thing as the wooden box that sat in my grandmother's kitchen dripping ice water into a pan. I may use the same name for both of them, but Sophie isn't fooled for an instant.

[Watching Our Language]

Deceptively Yours

I had a call from a friend, a Belgian linguist who does a lot of work on idioms in English and other languages. She asked me what I thought *on the up and up* meant. I told her it meant "above board" or "on the level," as in, "Are you sure these intelligence reports are on the up and up?"

"Does it mean anything else?" she asked.

"Not as far as I know," I told her.

"Not so fast," she said—"go look it up on the Web."

So I googled the phrase, and damned if more half of the first hundred hits for *on the up and up* didn't have it meaning "on the increase," or "improving," as in "Hong Kong's trade is on the up and up." True, a number of these came from sites in the UK and other foreign countries—it turns out the Brits have been using "on the up and up" like this for more than seventy years. (The Oxford English Dictionary entry for the phrase includes the sense "steadily rising, improving," but no American dictionary has cottoned to that sense.)

But I was surprised to see how many Americans use the expression that way, too. I found newspaper stories announcing that school activities fees were on the up and up in Minnesota, that sales were on the up and up for a Chicago publisher of datebooks, and that tourism was on the up and up on the Delmarva Penninsula. A defensive end for the Tampa Bay Bucs says that his career is "still on the up and up . . . still on the rise."

Out of curiosity, I sent a question about the expression to a discussion group that's populated by dialectologists and other devotees of word-lore. I had an e-mail back from someone in Berkeley who told me that he had been surprised to hear that *on the up and up* could be used to mean "on the increase." But when he asked his wife about it, she said that for her that was the only thing it could mean—she never knew it could mean "on the level." And what made it odder still was that they've been married for more than twenty years and both grew up in Southern California.

I had this image of the two of them sitting at the breakfast table. He asks, "Is your brother's new business on the up and up?" and she says, "No, but he's making do." And they go on like that with neither of them ever realizing that they're talking at cross-purposes. Deborah Tannen, call your office.

Of course expressions are always changing their meaning, and every once in a while one of those shifts trips the alarm of the usage patrols. But more often than not, these disparate meanings live side-by-side without anybody noticing. Not long ago, *The New York Times* quoted an Air Force major who disparaged the complaints made by American troops in Iraq: "I have real heartburn about the people you see on television griping about how they're stuck over there." I had always assumed that when *heartburn* is used metaphorically, it refers to anxiety or worry, but when I checked I found a lot of people using it to mean "anger" or "indignation"—"Cable's forced diet of programming is giving viewers heartburn"; "junk e-mail, a source of heartburn and anger for computer users everywhere." Is that the result of a difference in dialect or diet?

In fact sometimes a word can have contradictory meanings with no one being the wiser. I once got into an argument with a linguist friend over the meaning of the sentence "The pool was deceptively shallow." I maintained that it meant that the pool was shallower than it looked, and he said it meant that the pool was deeper than it looked. To settle the argument I took advantage of my role as chair of the usage panel of the *American Heritage Dictionary*, a group of 175 noted writers we poll every so often on usage questions. But when we asked the panelists what "The pool is deceptively shallow" means, the results were curiously inconclusive. Half of them said that it means "The pool is shallower than it appears," a third said that it means "The pool is deeper than it appears," and the rest said it could go either way. In other words, if you put that sentence on a warning sign you can be dead certain that anywhere from a third to a half of the people who see it will get the wrong message.

Or take *minimal*. "She ran best when she had a minimal amount of food in her stomach"—does that mean she ran best when she'd eaten nothing or when she'd eaten a bit? The usage panel was split on that one, too—a third said A, a third said B, and another third said it could mean either one.

If you're of a pessimistic turn of mind, you could take all this as a reminder of how elusive understanding can be—it puts us on guard against what Adrienne Rich called the dream of a common language. But maybe the wonder of it all is that we manage to muddle through, breakfast after breakfast, trusting to good faith to bridge over all the gaps in comprehension. To paraphrase another poet, Randall Jarrell: We understand each other worse, and it matters less, than any of us suppose.

The Bloody Crossroads of Grammar and Politics

Is there a grammatical error in the following sentence? *Toni Morrison's genius enables her to create novels that arise from and express the injustices African Americans have endured*. Not according to the Educational Testing Service, which included the item on the PSAT given on October 15 of last year. But Kevin Keegan, a high-school journalism teacher from Silver Spring, Maryland, protested that a number of grammar books assert that it is incorrect to use a pronoun with a possessive antecedent like "Tony Morrison's"—or at least, unless the pronoun is itself a possessive, as in *Toni Morrison's fans adore her books*.

After months of exchanges with the tenacious Keegan, the College Board finally agreed to adjust the scores of students who had marked the underlined pronoun *her* as incorrect. That's only fair. When you're asking students to pick out errors of grammar, you ought to make sure you haven't included anything that might bring the grammarati out of the woodwork.

Some read the test item as the token of a wider malaise. "Talk about standards," wrote David Skinner, a columnist at the conservative *Weekly Standard*. Not only had the example sentence been "proven to contain an error of grammar," but the sentence's celebration of Toni Morrison, a "mediocre contemporary author," betrayed the "faddish, racialist, wishful thinking that our educational institutions should be guarding against."

That may seem like a lot to lay on the back of a grammar example. But it was telling how easily Skinner's indignation encompassed both the grammatical and cultural implications of the sentence. In recent decades, the defense of usage standards has become a flagship issue for the cultural right: The people who are most vociferous about grammatical correctness tend to be those most dismissive of the political variety. And along the way, grammatical correctness itself has become an increasingly esoteric and arbitrary notion.

Take the rule about pronouns and possessives that Keegan cited in his challenge to the testing service. Unlike the hoary shibboleths about the split infinitive or beginning sentences with "but," this one is a relative newcomer, which seems to have surfaced in grammar books only in the 1960s. Wilson Follett endorsed it in his 1966 *Modern American Usage*, and it was then picked up by a number of other usage writers, including Jacques Barzun and John Simon.

The assumption behind the rule is that a pronoun has to be of the same part of speech as its antecedent. Since possessives are adjectives, the reasoning goes, they can't be followed by pronouns, even if the resulting sentence is perfectly clear.

If you accept that logic, you'll eschew sentences like *Napoleon's fame preceded him* (rewrite as *His fame preceded Napoleon*). In fact you'll have to take a red pencil to just about all of the great works of English literature, starting with Shakespeare and the King James Bible ("And Joseph's master took him, and put him into the prison"). The construction shows up in

Dickens and Thackeray, not to mention H. W. Fowler's *Modern English Usage* and in Strunk and White's *Elements of Style*, where we find "The writer's colleagues...have greatly helped him in the preparation of his manuscript." And it's pervasive not just in *The New York Times* and the *New Yorker*, but in the pages of the *Weekly Standard*, not excluding David Skinner's own columns. ("It may be Bush's utter lack of self-doubt that his detractors hate most about him.")

The ubiquity of those examples ought to put us on our guard—maybe the English language knows something that the usage writers don't. In fact the rule in question is a perfect example of muddy grammatical thinking. For one thing, possessives like *Mary's* aren't adjectives; they're what linguists call determiner phrases. (If you doubt that, try substituting *Mary's* for the adjective *happy* in sentences like *The child looks happy* or *We saw only healthy and happy children*.)

And if a nonpossessive pronoun can't have a possessive antecedent, logic should dictate that things can't work the other way around, either—if you're going to throw out *Hamlet's mother loved him*," then why accept *Hamlet loved his mother*? That's an awful lot to throw over the side in the name of consistency.

But that's what "correct grammar" often comes down to nowadays. It has been taken over by cultists who learned everything they needed to know about grammar in ninth grade, and who have turned the enterprise into an insider's game of gotcha! For those purposes, the more obscure and unintuitive the rule, the better. Pity the poor writers who come at grammar armed only with common sense and a knowledge of what English writers have done in the past. You're walking down the street minding your own business, and all of a sudden the grammar police swoop down and bust you for violating some ordinance you couldn't possibly have been aware of.

Not all modern usage writers take doctrinaire views of grammar. But the politicization of usage has contributed to its trivialization, and has vitiated it as an exercise in intellectual discrimination. The more vehemently people insist on upholding standards in general, the less need there is to justify them in the particular. For many, usage standards boil down to the unquestioned truths of "traditional grammar," even if some of the traditions turn out to be only a few decades old.

Take the way Skinner asserted that the College Board examination sentence was "proven to contain an error of grammar" in the way you might talk about a document being proven to be a forgery—it's as if the rules of grammar were mysterious dicta handed down from long-forgotten sages. For some writers, that's a natural pairing. The English conservative writer Roger Scruton has described the controversies over usage as merely a special case of the debate between conservative and liberal views of politics. But until fifty years ago, nobody talked about "conservative" and "liberal" positions on usage, and usage writers were drawn from both sides of the aisle.

Even today, it would be silly to claim that conservatives actually care more deeply about usage standards than liberals do, much less that they write more clearly or correctly. In language as elsewhere, it isn't as if vices are less prevalent among the people who denounce them most energetically.

But people who have reservations about the program of the cultural right often find themselves in an uneasy position when the discussion turns to usage. How do you defend the distinction between *disinterested* and *uninterested* without suggesting that its disappearance is a harbinger of the decline of the West? For that matter, how do you make the general case for standards when they're no longer answerable to common educated consent?

Not that the cultural left is blameless in this. Some of the usage reforms they championed have been widely adopted, and society is the better for it. There aren't a lot of male executives around who still refer to their secretaries as "my girl." But many of the locutions and usage rules that have recently been proposed in the name of social justice are as much insider codes as the arcane strictures of the grammar cultists—think of the *s/he* business, for example. They're exercises in moral fastidiousness that no one really expects will catch on generally.

To younger writers, a lot of these discussions of usage seem to be less about winning consensus than about winning points. It's no wonder they tend to regard the whole business with a weary indifference. WHAT-ever—will this be on the test?

Letter Perfect

TLAMs and RPGs, MREs and SSEs, EPWs and WMDs. The language we were hearing from the Iraq war had a decidedly alphabetic ring. But then that's only appropriate. The word "acronym" itself was first used exactly sixty years ago to describe military coinings like WAC, ANZAC, and *radar*, all drawn from the initials of longer phrases. By then, the process was familiar enough so that servicemen could make fun of it with the term *snafu*, for "situation normal, all fucked up." (*Snafu* was so successful that it gave rise to other phrases like *fubb*, for "fucked up beyond belief," and *cummfu* for "complete utter monumental military fuck-up." But none of these had legs except *fubar*, "fucked up beyond all recognition," which under the spelling *foobar* has survived as programmer's slang, though it's used now as a generic file name or command.)

True, the American fondness for acronyms and abbreviations dates from well before World War II. After all, ours was the first modern nation to be known by its initials—the abbreviation U.S. dates from the 1830s. Nineteenth-century Americans gave the language items like C.O.D., S.O.B., and P.D.Q., not to mention O.K.—certainly the most successful American contribution to the languages of the world, even if nobody's sure what the letters originally stood for.

It wasn't until the mid-twentieth century that acronyms became the linguistic wallpaper of modern life. One of the most successful acronyms of the 1950s was *veep*, which was used affectionately for Truman's vice president Alban Barkley. It was largely abandoned in 1953 when Richard Nixon took over the job and made it known that he didn't like the appellation—Nixon wasn't a man for whom the phrase "lighten up" had a lot of resonance. But the Republican administration compensated by introducing other acronyms like *riff* for "reduction in force." That was the first bureaucratic euphemism for layoffs—and as it turns out, a surprisingly resilient one.

Some sticklers insist that *acronym* should only be used for a string of letters that's pronounced as a word, like *riff* or NATO—items like FBI and LSD they call initialisms. I suppose that's a valid distinction, but most people can't be bothered with it, and anyway, it misses the main point. However they're pronounced, the crucial thing about these expressions is the way they come to live lives of their own as separate words. AC in a real-estate classified ad is just an abbreviation for "air conditioning." But AC/DC is a distinct word when it's used to describe a sexual orientation—if you heard someone's sexuality described as "alternating current/direct current" your thoughts would run in a very different direction. And you may have your doubts about UFOs, but no one denies the existence of unidentified flying objects.

It's astonishing how pervasive these coinings have become over the past sixty years. I'm not thinking just of the ones that come from bureaucracy and technology. Those are mostly used for efficiency—strings like SEC and EEG flow a lot more trippingly from the tongue than Securities and Exchange Commission and electroencephalogram.

But by now acronyms are piled up in every room in the American house. BLTs, PB&Js and OJ in the kitchen; GTOs, RVs, and SUVs in the garage, and TP in the bathroom, proving that someone remembered to stop at the A&P. In the living room we turn on the VCR or put on a CD by REM, ELO, or UB40; in the bedroom we slip out of our BVDs and cop some Zs. Yuppies and WASPS, LSD and PCP, TGIF and BYOB, CBGBs and MTV—you could sketch the social history of the postwar period just by listing the initials it has carved on the walls.

Items like these don't have much to do with a propensity for conciseness—in fact most of them barely save any syllables over their spelled-out equivalents. The urge to acronymize goes deeper than that. It's as if we're moving towards a purely analytic language, where the shape of every word reveals its meaning to the initiates who possess the secret key. There's a profane manifestation of that urge in the stories people tell about how our most charged words are secret acronyms derived from phrases like "For Unlawful Carnal Knowledge"—a bit of linguistic folklore that seems impervious to philological correction.

In that sense, acronyms are the slang of a textual world. There's a mysterious sense of destiny to these names. The cabalists used the process called notarikon to form new names for God by combining the first or last letters of the words from phrases or biblical verses. And the Tudors studded their verses with acronyms and acrostics—though probably not nearly as many as scholars have claimed to find in their efforts to prove that Shakespeare's works were written by someone else.

That's the same impulse that leads people to rig the game—they start with a plausible acronym and then contrive a description to fit it. As best I can tell, the first of these was WAVES, the name the Navy coined in 1942 for "Women Accepted for Volunteer Emergency Service," a description that managed to be simultaneously condescending and inaccurate. In later years the same process has given us organizational names like CARE, NOW, and MADD.

No one is more adept at this game than legislators. Over the past few years we've had the RAVE Act, for "Reducing Americans' Vulnerability to Ecstasy," and operation TIPS, the Terrorism Information and Prevention System. And then there's the antiterrorism act that goes by the name of "Uniting and Strengthening America by Providing Appropriate Tools Required to Intercept and Obstruct Terrorism." That acronymizes as USA PATRIOT—a happy accident indeed.

A Thousand Pictures

Some years ago, I inherited a seven-volume set of the 1907 Grand Larousse French dictionary. The set is pretty tattered by now, but it's still glorious, with its dark red covers embossed with trees and gold letters, its art nouveau frontispieces and letter pages, and above all its intricate engravings and maps and its resplendent color plates—plates of animals, birds and insects; plates of costumes and furniture; plates of eggs, locomotives, and fencing positions; and lots and lots of plates of military uniforms.

That's the dictionary that Jean-Paul Sartre recounts reading as a child in his grandfather's study in Alsace, in his autobiographical novel *Les Mots*:

> The *Grand Larousse* was everything to me; I would take down a volume at random, behind the desk, on the next-to-last shelf. A-bello, belloc-Ch, or Ci-D ... (these associations of syllables had become proper names that denoted the sectors of universal knowledge: there was the Ci-D region, the Pr-Z region, with their flora and fauna, their cities, their great men and their battles). ... Men and beasts were there in person—the engravings were their bodies, the text was their souls, their unique essences.

Fresh Air Commentary, August 7, 2003

An American child isn't likely to have that experience of the dictionary nowadays. For all their considerable virtues, most of our dictionaries aren't books to take us lands away. The average dictionary may include a handful of color plates, but it's basically a textual affair—the illustrations serve mostly to break the unrelieved monotony of the columns of type. Those dictionaries do fine on souls, but there's not a lot to satisfy our hunger for bodies.

Still, even those dictionaries have their visual charms, and it was nice to see a piece in the Sunday *New York Times Magazine* on Jeffrey Middleton, who's the illustrator of the new eleventh edition of Merriam-Webster's Collegiate. Middleton is responsible for the elegant little pen-and-ink drawings inserted every couple of pages or so alongside the entries, in a style that hasn't much changed in the past seventy-five years.

Dictionary traditionalists argue that those drawings do a better job of rendering the idea of a word than elaborate plates or photographs. As the noted lexicographer Sidney Landau once put it, "Photographs are necessarily of unidealized individual things, whether zebras, geese, or medieval churches, [whereas] drawings may represent a composite distillation."

Actually, that remark says as much about our conception of photography as it does about dictionaries. It's a fair bet that Pierre Larousse would have used photographs in his grand dictionary if he'd had the technology to print them properly. In that age, people didn't have any problem thinking of photographs as the representations of abstract ideas or imaginary settings. Victorian photographers like Oscar Rejlander and Henry Peach Robinson produced staged allegories and dramatic scenes with titles like "Youth and Age" or "The Two Ways of Life." Julia Cameron did photographic illustrations for Tennyson's "Idylls of the King," and Henry James allowed the use of photographs to illustrate a 1909 edition of *The Golden Bowl*. And Darwin's cousin Francis Galton made composite photographs aimed at isolating the physiognomic traits of various types and classes—criminals, Jews, and the members of the Academy of Sciences.

In that age, abstraction was an accepted goal of photography— in the words of the critic Charles Caffin, a collaborator of Alfred Stieglitz: "the artist [photographer] must make some abstract quality the prime feature of his picture." It wasn't until the early twentieth century that people began to think of photography as a pure record of the concrete facts before the lens. For Paul Strand, Andre Kertesz, and Henri Cartier-Bresson, there could be no photographs but of things. As Strand once said, "[T]he camera machine cannot evade the objects that are in front of it."

Within a few decades, the notion of photographing abstract ideas brought to mind the kitschy propaganda photos that the Nazis and Soviets made, with titles like "Sunday Volunteers" or "The Next Generation." And modernists might allow you to make a film of a novel, but you couldn't use stills from it as illustrations when the book was reissued.

So it's understandable that a lot of modern lexicographers should hold that a photograph can only represent a particular badger, not the idea of badgerhood. And even today no American dictionary uses photographs to illustrate the meanings of words apart from the *American Heritage*. (I should say that I'm associated with that dictionary, though they keep me pretty far from the art department end of things.)

Yet contemporary photographers put those austere modernist scruples behind them some time ago. Fabulists like Joel Peter Witkin, surrealists like Sandy Skoglund, narrative photographers like Tina Barney—all of them take the object in front of the lens as standing in for something other than itself. I like to imagine some avant-garde *Grand Larousse* of the future that's illustrated with modern photographs like Cindy Sherman's depictions of herself in the guise of a housewife or a Raphael, or the photographs that Laurie Simmons calls "Food," "Clothing," and "Shelter," where figurines of leggy women wear hot dogs, gloves, and houses on their upper bodies like the dancing cigarette packs in the Old Gold commercials of the fifties.

But the problem with the way most modern dictionaries are illustrated isn't just what they imply about photographs, but what they imply about words. They leave you with the impression that words are colorless abstractions at an eternal remove from the concrete realm of the senses. You think of the angels in Wim Wender's *Wings of Desire*, who float in black and white above the streets of Berlin and never make contact with sensory experience. Yet when you hear words like *bagel* or *bullfrog*, what comes to mind isn't a sketchy silhouette. Meanings are part of the world, too, and they have color and texture just like everything else. You can even take pictures of them.

All That You Can Bee

Mark Twain held that the ability to spell well was an inborn talent like a photographic memory—"The spelling faculty is born in man, like poetry, music and art. It is a gift; it is a talent." If that's true, God seems to have distributed the gift in a scrupulously even-handed way, with no regard for more general intellectual capacities. Or at least that's what I like to think, being one of the mass of people who are chronically shaky on the difference between -*ible* and -*able*.

Americans have always placed a singular importance on spelling. In fact the spelling bee was the original American game show, and often the only entertainment in town. It was born in colonial times, when the attainment of correct spelling was regarded as a symbol of cultivation. Back then the contests were called "spelling schools" or "spelling matches." Horace Greeley reminisced fondly about his successes as a spelling prodigy when he was a boy in New Hampshire around 1815—as he put it, spelling was a natural strength for "a child of tenacious memory and no judgment." And whatever Mark Twain's reservations about the value of spelling, he prided himself on having been a champion speller as a youth in Missouri: "I always slaughtered

Fresh Air Commentary, May 14, 2003

both divisions and stood alone with the medal around my neck when the campaign was finished."

By the mid-nineteenth century, the contests had become an adult pastime, as well. Bret Harte recounted a spelling competition in the California mining camps that ended in a fight with bowie knives when two contestants disagreed over whether "eider-duck" began with an *i* or an *e*. That may have been a tall tale, but contemporary letters document the popularity of spelling bees in the camps.

The phrase "spelling bee" itself entered the language in the 1870s, when the competitions became a popular mass entertainment. (The OED derives that use of *bee* from the name of the insect, but it's more likely related to the English dialect word *been*, which referred to "voluntary help given by neighbors toward the accomplishment of a particular task.") More than 4,000 people attended one bee at the Philadelphia Academy of Music in 1875, and a disturbance broke out when the audience judged that one contestant had been unfairly eliminated for misspelling *receipt*.

After a period of eclipse, the bees were revived again in the 1920s as a way of encouraging the civic virtues of literacy among schoolchildren—one enthusiast described them as "an antidote to jazz and frivolity." The first national bee was held in 1925, and for the last sixty years the event has been sponsored by Scripps-Howard.

Jeff Blitz's *Spellbound* is an engaging and surprisingly moving documentary that follows the fortunes of eight contestants in the 1999 national bee held in Washington, D.C. Some of the kids are motivated by pure competitive spirit, but for most of them, the bee stands for the struggle to move up and on in American life.

Angela is a Texas girl whose father came to America from Mexico as an undocumented immigrant. He still speaks no English, and his trip to Washington to watch his daughter compete in the national seems to seal his life's accomplishment. Ashley is a black girl from the Washington, D.C., projects who describes herself as a "prayer warrior." And Neil from San Clemente, California, is the son of a successful Indian immigrant with a boundless faith in the American dream. "In America," the father says, "If you work hard, you'll make it."

The kids are all bright and winning and incredibly dedicated, and you feel their anguish as they're eliminated one after the other, in a cruel prototype of *Survivor*. But while that experience would have been familiar to Greeley or Twain, neither of them would have been likely to prevail in a modern competition. Back in the first decades of the national competition, the contestants were given the sorts of words that an ordinary literate citizen would be expected to know, like *promiscuous, intelligible*, and *fracas*. In 1932, Dorothy Greenwald from Des Moines, Iowa, walked away with the laurels when she was able to spell *knack*. But like a lot of other competitive events, the spelling bee has become a lot more specialized and intense over the course of time. In recent years the winning words in the national bee have included such bower-bird treasures as *xanthosis, vivisepulture, euonym, succedaneum*, and *prospicience*.

That inevitably changes the significance of the exercise. God may have given some people a gift for spelling, but He almost certainly didn't intend that it should extend to getting *succedaneum* right. At this level, in fact, the competition isn't really about the capriciousness of English spelling. It has more to do with the indistinctness of English pronunciation, which merges *p*'s and *b*'s and *t*'s and *d*'s, and which reduces every unstressed vowel to a blurry "uh." That isn't much of an impediment when the word is one you already recognize, like *intelligible* or *fracas*. But it makes it impossible to pin down the spelling of an unfamiliar word, particularly when its derivation is obscure. In fact I often had the feeling that the pronouncer was making an effort to keep the pronunciations as uninformative and ambiguous as possible.

You can sense the contestants' perplexity as the pronouncer feeds them words like *apocope*, *hellebore*, *clavecin*, and *alegar*—items that most people can happily live their lives without ever encountering. Occasionally the kids' faces brighten when they recognize a word that happens to be on their cram lists, but usually they're reduced to mere guessing. I felt a special sympathy for the kid who was eliminated when he blew *opsimath*, a word for someone who begins learning late in life. "O-B-S-O . . . ," he started, not recognizing *opsi-* as the Greek root for "late"—as anyone would know who sees the connection to that other household word *opsigamy*.

Yet even if spelling ability isn't a very good indicator of intellectual capacity, you have no doubt that most of the kids profiled in *Spellbound* will succeed in later life. America still rewards dedication and hard work, just as it did in Horace Greeley's day. And the modern spelling bee rewards something else: You have to have an instinct for understanding indistinct commands to perform arbitrary and often pointless acts, and somehow figure out what's expected of you. In today's America, that's another talent that serves you well.

Like, Wow!

I had been thinking about the word *like*, so I was listening for it in all the press interviews with students after the school shootings near San Diego last week. Understandably, most of them were struggling to put their thoughts in words, and their speech was punctuated by *um*s and *er*s and *you know*s. But of the dozen students that I listened to, not one used the word *like*. Nobody said, "Like, they were yelling at us to leave the building" or "I was like, 'let's get out of here.'"

There's no question that all these kids use *like* that way in their ordinary conversation—you'd be hard-pressed to find a dozen adolescents in the whole country who don't. But whatever critics and teachers may think, *like* is more than just an unconscious tic or a filler that people stick in while they're vamping for time. It's a word with a point of view, and speakers can shut it down when that isn't what they want to convey.

Like a lot of modern sensibilities, that point of view and that use of *like* originated with the hipsters of the fifties. In their mouths, it wasn't a sign of inarticulateness, the way people would come to think of it later. Nobody ever accused the hipsters of being at a loss for words, even if it wasn't always easy to know

Fresh Air Commentary, March 20, 2001

what they meant. But the word contributed to the sense of a language that didn't actually mean anything so much as it evoked, the way a jazz riff does. It turned everything the hipsters said into a kind of extended simile, as if to say, "I, like, gotta use words when I talk to you."

Mainstream Americans didn't learn that kind of talk from the hipsters themselves. They got it from TV and radio programs that diffused the lingo in a diluted form. DJ's like Wolfman Jack and Philadelphia's Hy Lit lifted their patter from the comic Lord Buckley, who also originated the hipster shtick that Steve Allen worked over in his bopster fairy tales. Sid Caesar had a bopster character called Progress Hornsby, and Lenny Bruce did a much more dead-on routine in the persona of jazz musician Shorty Peterstein. And probably most influentially, at least in the culture at large, there was Maynard G. Krebs, the goateed beatnik wannabe that Bob Denver played on the late-fifties TV show *The Many Loves of Dobie Gillis*. Krebs was given to saying things on the order of "Like, wow! That is, like, really, like, cool!"

To a lot of adults in those days, that was pretty much the way all teenagers were starting to sound. In short measure, critics were making *like* the symptom of an alarming decline in communication skills among the nation's young people. That single word seemed to embody all the pernicious influences at work in the culture—lax standards, television, poor manners, and a spreading mindlessness. And it's true that the teenagers who picked up on *like* seemed to use it indiscriminately. But there was method in it—one way or another, *like* lays a certain distance between speakers and their words. Sometimes it can soften a request, as in "Could I, like, borrow your sweater?" Sometimes it communicates disaffection: "Whaddawe suppose to, like, read this?" Or you can use it to nod ironically at the banality of your words, as in, "Do you suppose we could, like, talk about it?" That's one use of the word that just about everybody has picked up on; I even use it in e-mail.

However *like* is used, though, you can still hear faint echoes of the hipster, at least in the sense that the word suggests the expressive limits of description. That might explain why young people in the eighties started to use the word as what linguists call a quotative marker, as in "I was like, 'That is so uncool.'" The construction first came to national attention in 1982, when Moon Unit Zappa used it in her song *Valley Girl*, and it was quickly stereotyped as adolescent female speech, though in fact boys probably use it as much as girls do. Not surprisingly, that use of the word set in motion another wave of denunciations from critics who wondered why teenagers couldn't say "I said" instead of "I was like." But those aren't the same. What follows "I said" is a report of people's words; what follows "I was like" is a performance of their actions. That's why "I was like" is as apt to be followed by a noise or gesture as by a sentence. *Say* is for telling, *like* is for showing.

It's no wonder *like* has become one of the linguistic emblems of the age. No other word embodies so many of the sensibilities that have been converging in the language since the hipsters first made their appearance—the ironizing, the mistrust of description, and particularly, the way we look to drama and simulation to do the work that used to be done by narrative. As Raymond Williams once observed, "We have never as a society acted so much or watched so many others acting." In fact the average person hears more drama in any given week than an Elizabethan would have seen in an entire lifetime, back in what we think of as the Golden Age of drama. The dramatization isn't limited to movies and TV sitcoms. It spills over to the cheerful exchanges of the happy talk news shows and the radio ads that can only make their point in little dialogues: "And that's not all, Stan—I learned that I can pay off my new storm windows in easy installments."

In the midst of all that theatricality, it's silly to get all huffy when the language comes up with a new construction that sets the scene for our dramatizings. Anyway, language doesn't fix our mindset nearly as tyrannically as people like to think it does. When those kids down in San Diego County were faced with talking about the school shootings, they had no use for *like* and the distance it would have interposed between them and their words. They know as well as anybody that there are times when you have to throw yourself back on narrative to make sense of things.

Lucubratin' Rhythm

I picked up a copy of *Commentary* a while ago, and there was Norman Podhoretz deploring the national obsession with sexual
harassment, a concern that he tracked to what he called "the
arcane lucubrations of marginal academics." That word *lucubration* seems to be a favorite of waspish critics who want to deflate
the pretensions of artists, intellectuals, and other people they
consider self-important. John Simon used it to describe Wallace
Shawn's plays, James Kirkpatrick used it of the editorials in the
New York Times, and the literary critic Joseph Epstein complained
about "the opaque lucubrations of structuralists, semioticists and
deconstructionists."

The wonder is that the word is still around. It originally
comes from the Latin for "work by lamp light," and refers to
laborious study, or more generally to any writing that's learned
or pretentious. I first looked up the word a number of years ago,
when I ran into it in one of Dr. Johnson's essays—that's the nice
thing about recondite words like *lucubrate*: You can have precise
memories of your first encounters with them. But it was clearly
a rare and mock-pompous word even back in the eighteenth century. And by all rights, it should have disappeared when English
gave up trying to refashion itself as a dialect of Latin. It should
have gone the way of *clancular*, *cubiculary*, *deuteroscopy*, and

other latinate mouthfuls that Johnson included in his *Dictionary*.

For some reason, though, *lucubration* has managed to cling to life in the penumbra of the English vocabulary, maybe because it smacks of the very pedantry it usually describes. I've never actually written the word before now; I've always thought of it as one of those items that you're better off just taking a quiet pride in knowing. But I can understand the urge to stick it in. It's a fine-sounding string of syllables: You have the feeling that whatever *lucubrate* denotes, it's probably a very good name for it. And as a word like that gets increasingly rarefied, it naturally tends to slip from its moorings and drift off on a plane of pure sound-symbolism. Carried away on the assonance of those *u*'s, people start to use *lucubration* to mean all sorts of things. Sometimes it seems to mean just "ramblings" or "banalities," and sometimes it seems to mean something like "rummaging around."

Even the redoubtable William F. Buckley used *lucubrate* incorrectly as a transitive verb when he described the defense attorneys in the O. J. Simpson trial as "lucubrating a defense thesis." I expect that Buckley meant something like "dreaming up" or "conjuring." But you can be sure that Dr. Johnson would never have used the verb with a direct object—you could lucubrate *on* a defense, but that would have a different meaning. And there was an even more startling malapropism in a review of a Tom Wolfe novel that Norman Mailer published in the *New York Review of Books*. It contained the sentence

> No one will ever be the same after reading [Wolfe's] set piece on the massive copulation of a prize stallion with a thoroughbred mare (after she has been readied for this momentous event by the lucubrations produced in her by the mouth and nose of a third horse, Sad Sam!).

I don't know exactly what Mailer imagined was going on in the mare, but it presumably wasn't scholarly musings. Probably he was misled by the resemblance to *lubrication* and *lubricious*. But it's notable that the gaffe eluded the editors as well.

When William F. Buckley, Norman Mailer, and the editors of the *New York Review of Books* have all lost their grip on the meaning of a word, maybe we should think about putting it out to pasture. And while we're at it, there are other Johnsonian holdovers that we might want to give notice to, like *lambent, etiolated, tergiversation, rebarbative,* and *jejune. (Jejune* in particular is almost always a bad idea.)

Of course the second you propose dropping a word like *lucubration,* the Friends of the English Language will be up in arms to remind you of our obligation to preserve all the fine distinctions and shades of meaning that have been handed down to us. But those were gone long ago. It isn't just that most people don't have any context for a word like *lucubration,* but that whatever nuances it might have had once are washed out now by the pure resplendence of its syllables. When a word starts to sound that elegant, nobody can hear what it's saying anymore.

I know that none of this is going to stanch the urge to use these words. They may annoy or puzzle most of the people who read them, but then when you see somebody using a word like *lucubration* or *lambent,* you can be pretty sure that it wasn't stuck in for the reader's benefit in the first place. And sometimes you have to forgive a writer for indulging a love of big words, particularly when they're as delectable a mouthful as *lucubration* is—and even if, unlike Dr. Johnson, they're not flogging a dictionary on the side. But let's face it: That isn't communication, it's gargling.

Ain't Misbehavin'

Exactly forty years ago the *New Yorker* ran a cartoon by Alan Dunn that showed a receptionist at the Merriam-Webster company saying to a visitor: "Sorry, Dr. Gove ain't in." You'd have to have a pretty long memory to get that reference today. But at the time, most *New Yorker* readers would have known that the Dr. Gove in question was Philip Gove, the editor of Merriam-Webster's massive *Third New International Dictionary*, which had been published a few months earlier.

By any standard, Webster's *Third* was a monumental work of scholarship. But it stirred up a storm of controversy over what people considered its "permissive" approach to usage. More than anything else, what outraged the critics was that the dictionary declined to label *ain't* as colloquial or substandard, noting that even cultivated people often used the word in speech as a contraction of "am not" and "is not."

That was all it took to open the floodgates. *The New York Times* described the dictionary as a bolshevik document, and the Chicago *Daily News* took it as the symptom of "a general decay in values." A columnist for the Toronto *Telegram* called the dictionary's acceptance of *ain't* a shameful business—"It is one of

Fresh Air Commentary, September 18, 2002

the ugliest words in the English language, and I want no part of it."

Those fulminations sound a little over the top today, but then, this was thirty years before the phrase "lighten up" entered the language. Nowadays nobody blinks when dictionaries list words like *yadda-yadda*—in fact there's probably nothing a new dictionary could include that could cause a major national scandal, certainly not to the point of inspiring a cartoon in the *New Yorker*. Yet *ain't* is no closer to being standard English than it was then. In the upstairs-downstairs world of language, *ain't* is still required to use the servants' entrance.

There has always been something odd about the stigma attached to *ain't*. The word has been around since the seventeenth century, and for a long time nobody thought it was worse than any other contraction. Writers from Swift to Tennyson used it in their letters and speech in a completely unselfconscious way, and so did a number of Jane Austen characters. It wasn't until the middle of the nineteenth century that critics started to condemn the word, and made the avoidance of ain't the emblem of middle-class linguistic fastidiousness. The English upper class hung on to it for a while longer—Winston Churchill regularly used it in conversation, and Dorothy Sayers was always putting it into the mouth of her aristocratic sleuth Lord Peter Wimsey. But by the time Webster's *Third* appeared, not even nobs were using the word in earnest.

It's hard to see what makes *ain't* more objectionable than any other contraction, particularly when it's short for "am not." The aversion to "ain't I" is so strong that people have invented the absurdly ungrammatical "aren't I" as an alternative. ("Aren't I? I sure are.") That's a pretty desperate expedient just to avoid using *ain't*, and grammarians from H. W. Fowler to William Safire have urged that it's time for "ain't I" be accepted as standard English.

Even with dictionaries and grammarians pleading for its rehabilitation, it isn't likely that *ain't* will be allowed into the drawing room of the language any time soon. I suspect that this isn't just because educated people disapprove of *ain't* in other people's speech, but because they find it so useful in their own.

Educated speakers have always used *ain't* when they feel like a little linguistic slumming. But in recent years I'm hearing them use it more and more in a different way, when they want to suggest that a fact is just obvious on the face of things. A while ago a friend sent me an article from the *Chronicle of Higher Education* that quoted a dean at a prestigious Eastern university: "Any junior scholar who pays attention to teaching at the expense of research ain't going to get tenure." That *ain't* was a nice touch, I thought. It made it clear that the dean's conclusion wasn't based on expert knowledge or some recent committee report—it was something that should be clear to anyone with an ounce of sense.

That's the message that *ain't* conveys in all those common expressions like "It ain't over till the fat lady sings" or "If it ain't broke, don't fix it"—*ain't* tells you that you're dealing with a nitty-gritty verity that you don't need a college education to understand. The language is full of sayings that use *ain't* like that, and they'd lose their proletarian pizzazz if you tried to put them in standard English: "It is not necessarily so," "You have not seen anything yet," "Hit them where they aren't," "That is not hay," "Is that not a shame?"

But educated people couldn't keep using *ain't* that way if the word weren't considered a mark of uneducated speech. And it turns out that educated people use the word an awful lot. There are more than four million Web pages containing *ain't*, virtually all of them put there by authors who know full well that the word isn't supposed to be standard English. It gives you a sense of why everyone has such an interest in keeping *ain't* from becoming a respectable linguistic citizen—what would we use to do our dirty work?

There Are No Postmodernists in a Foxhole

Like a lot of my favorite stories, this one has a pronoun in a featured role. It began with an article in the *Chronicle of Higher Education* that quoted Harvard President Lawrence Summers saying, "I regret any faculty member leaving a conversation feeling they are not respected."

The sentence was tailor-made to bundle puristic panties, particularly given the context and speaker—and in fact a few weeks later, the *Chronicle* ran an extensive diatribe from a professor of English who took exception to Summers' grammar. According to the writer, Summers should have said "I regret any faculty member's leaving," not "any faculty member leaving." And the antecedent "any faculty member" required the pronouns "he or she," not "they." (Modern academics are particularly attached to the "he or she" construction, which enables them to sound politically correct and pedantic in the same breath.)

The writer went on to chide President Summers for contributing to the general decline of precision in language—all the more distressing in someone who has presented himself as a crusader for scholarly rigor. Indeed, he said, the woeful state of the language is evident to anyone who listens to National Public

Fresh Air Commentary, August 20, 2002

Radio for fifteen minutes or reads a single section of *The New York Times*. That's what happens when students are taught that writing is a form of pure self-expression, the letter-writer claimed, so that students "need never accept correction; for if it is their precious little selves they are expressing, the language of expression is answerable only to the internal judgment of those same selves." We've come to the point, the writer said, where composition teachers have a horror of acting as language police and grammar itself is regarded as a form of reactionary tyranny.

The response went on in this vein for a full 1,750 words, and concluded with an insistence that all college composition courses should henceforth teach grammar and rhetoric and nothing else. In short, it was an utterly routine grammatical harangue, distinguished only by the speciousness of the occasion for it. For example, that business about having to use the possessive "any member's leaving" instead of "any member leaving" is one of those mindless superstitions that have been passed on to generations of schoolchildren at the end of Sister Petra's ruler. As the linguist Geoff Pullum pointed out in a letter to the *Chronicle*, if you really believed the construction was incorrect, you'd have to take the matter up with Shakespeare, Milton, Jane Austen, and most of the other great figures of English literature. As for the plural pronoun *they*, bear in mind that Summers's words were quoted from a spoken interview, and that everybody uses the plural that way in their informal speech.

In fact the only thing that made this disquisition notable is that its author was the redoubtable Stanley Fish, the literary theorist and self-styled champion of postmodern thought. As it happens, in fact, Fish's piece in the *Chronicle of Higher Education* appeared about the same time as another extended public pronouncement of his, this one in the July issue of *Harper's* magazine, where Fish offered a rejoinder to the attacks on postmodernism from the cultural right.

That anti-postmodernist jihad has been waged with particular ferocity since September 11, 2001, as the right invokes the terrorist attacks in an effort to score a decisive victory in the culture wars. The first salvo was fired just ten days after the attacks by Edward Rothstein in the *New York Times*'s culture pages. According to Rothstein, postmodernists would be unable to condemn the attacks in an unqualified way, since they reject universal values and ideals. In fact, he said, postmodernism leads to establishing a moral symmetry between the terrorist and his opponent. And *U.S. News & World Report* commentator John Leo warned that our campus cultures have been captured by "the postmodern conviction that there are no truths or moral norms worth defending." The result of that, he says, is an anything-goes morality and a "drumbeat of rule-breaking" that drowns out traditional values.

Now you don't have to be a devotee of academic fashion to see that this is all claptrap. In his *Harper's* article, Fish rightly pointed out that the "postmodernism" that the conservatives are attacking is a caricature of what he and others have actually argued. Listening to cultural conservatives talk about "postmodernists" nowadays, you're reminded of how the Church used to talk about the Masons.

Distortions aside, though, the attacks on postmodern doctrine are bizarre on the face of things. Granted, a lot of modern academic theorizing is flaky and pretentious—though anyone who thinks this is a new development ought to take a look at what Dwight Macdonald was saying about academic writing forty years ago. If conservative critics seriously believe that the moral order of America is threatened by its literature professors, they should get back on their meds. It isn't simply that the enterprises of philosophy and literary study have always been inconsequential in American life, and even in the American academy. More to the point, there's no group more deeply invested in traditional standards and cultural hierarchy than academic humanists are, whatever theory they drive to work.

When you read Fish's linguistic screed in the *Chronicle of Higher Education* it becomes immediately clear just how absurd the whole campaign against postmodernism has been. "No norms worth defending"? "Drumbeats of rule-breaking"? "One standard is as good as another"? Not on Stanley Fish's watch! When it comes to the crunch, Fish has ideas about standards that are every bit as conventional—and in the main, as unconsidered—as anything the cultural right could wish for. And most of his fellow-travelers will readily endorse those values, even if they might not pursue the point quite so splenetically. Not to worry: The future of the Republic is in safe hands.

Adverbially Yours

The other day I was listening to a colleague describe a piece of
software he'd built that produces automatic summaries of newspaper articles. It picks out the most topical sentences, then it
shortens them by stripping off their excess verbiage. "Like what?"
I asked. "Well, for one thing," he said, "we leave out the adverbs."
I pointed out that there are some adverbs that make a useful contribution to the meaning of a sentence. Words like *never* and *not*
come to mind—you wouldn't want an automatic summarizer to
come back with a precis of a presidential press conference that
read, "I had sexual relations with that woman."

Even so, I took his point. I recall hearing my eighth-grade
English teacher say that the most beautiful sentence in English is
"Jesus wept," because it doesn't say "Jesus wept bitterly." At the
time I didn't realize that this was just his opinion—I thought it
was some widely accepted judgment. But it's true a lot of sentences are improved when you take the adverbs out. Graham
Greene once said that if he opened a novel and someone
answered tenderly, he closed it immediately. And once the whole
of English literature is living online, maybe somebody will do us
a favor by setting loose a virus that erases all the instances of *tenderly* and *bitterly*, not to mention *plaintively*, *affectingly*, and *buoy-*

antly. As an editor friend of mine used to say, "Don't romance me, just pour the drink."

Adverbs tend to show people at their worst—posturing, embellishing, apologizing, or just being mealy-mouthed. Adverbs may be a relatively small proportion of the English vocabulary, but they account for about half the words on my personal enemies list. There are the lily-gilders like *significantly* and *aggressively*. Corporate publicists try to get at least one of these into every press release, almost always in a split infinitive: "We continue to aggressively reduce our cost base"; "We aim to significantly accelerate our delivery of products." Intensifiers like that always strike me as sad tokens of the anxiety that won't let people leave well enough alone.

Then there are the rain-check adverbs like *arguably*, which give us license to make extravagant claims on credit. Sports writers love *arguably.* If you read through one month's worth of *Sports Illustrated* recently, you would have learned that Simon Gagne is arguably the Philadelphia Flyers's best forward, that the Mets' Glendon Rusch is arguably the league's best number five starting pitcher, and that Mookie Wilson's tenth-inning appearance in game six of the 1986 World Series was arguably the greatest at-bat in Series history. Now I'll grant you that's one of the pleasures of talking sports, having endless arguments about superlatives that nobody can ever resolve. But there's no excuse when *Time* magazine claims in its election coverage last fall that "Education is arguably the nation's biggest problem." That may be true, but then you could say the same thing about health care, the environment, violence, or drugs. Maybe we could just say that education is a big national problem, and save the argument for deciding who's the best set-up man in the National League.

As long as we're driving *arguably* into the sea, perhaps we could also lose *quite possibly*. This one is a favorite of advertisers, who use it to drape their hyperbole with affected diffidence. "Quite possibly, the world's perfect food"; "Quite possibly the finest motorcoach ever built." It manages to be unctuous, grandiose, and suspicious at the same time, like a snooty butler who has been pocketing the silverware.

Adverbs do have their partisans; Henry James said that he adored them. And there are some that have gotten a bad rap through no fault of their own, like *hopefully*. Usage critics are always jumping on this one, but it does journeyman work for us. I recently heard a TV reporter talking about floods in Iowa. He said, "Hopefully, the waters will soon subside." I didn't see how else he could have put that. "I hope the waters will subside"? Well, but who cares what he hopes? "One hopes?" or "It is to be hoped ... "? Maybe a little stiff for cable news. Let's hang on to *hopefully*—it's a credit to its syntactic category.

But for the most part, when you see an adverb rounding the corner you have reasonable cause to stop and frisk. One thing I've noticed over the years is how songs with adverbs as their titles are usually sodden with lyrical bathos. "The evening breeze caressed the trees, tenderly." Or Stephen Stills's "Helplessly Hoping," the quintessential example of rock-lyric overreaching. And then there's *Suddenly*, an adverbial anthem that was a modest hit for Ray Peterson in 1960:

> *Suddenly, I fell so suddenly.*
> *Oh, and desperately, I wanted you so desperately,*
> *And if you'll be true to me, I'll love you tenderly.*

But there are some great adverb songs, too, like Billie Holiday's *Carelessly* and Brook Benton's *Endlessly*. Whatever its shortcomings as a suffix, *-ly* is a great syllable to croon.

Wed the People

In an interview last December, Howard Dean explained that Vermont had chosen to allow same-sex couples to enter into "civil unions" rather than "marriages" because "marriage is very important to a lot of people who are pretty religious." That led George Will to complain that Dean was reducing the debate over the public meaning of *marriage* to "merely a semantic quibble."

It's odd the way you always see *semantic* flanked by words like *merely* and *quibble*, even from writers who live by language. It's the posture of people who like to pretend they don't have the time or patience to bandy words.

But the dispute over marriage is as purely semantic as they come, particularly in a society as obsessed with words as ours is. We may like to pretend that we're a people with no patience for quibbling over "mere semantics," but not even the medievals of Pierre Abélard's age spent as much time as we do chewing over the nuances of names, symbols, labels, and titles. Hence our predilection for formulas like "the A-word," "the B-word" and so on, as every issue is reduced to a single controversial expression, from abortion, AIDS, and amnesty to Zionism and zoning.

What people have taken to calling "the M-word" is more

charged than most, because it's what linguists and philosophers call a performative notion. Like christening a boat or adjourning a meeting, marriage is a state of affairs that can be brought about merely by pronouncing certain words in an appropriate setting—words that have traditionally conferred not just solemn rights and obligations, but permission to canoodle, too.

But our anti-semantic postures can make it hard to come clean about our semantic preoccupations. That may be why opponents of gay marriage often appeal to slippery slope arguments, as if altering the meaning of the M-word will threaten "the institution of marriage" itself. That phrase doesn't simply evoke other bulwarks of the social order that we describe as institutions, like the free press and Dick Clark. It also blurs the distinction between the concept of marriage and its actuality. For opponents, broadening the definition of marriage is like opening an exclusive hotel to package tours, with the risk that the traditional clientele will no longer feel like checking in. It amounts to "taking the rights and protection of marriage and handing them out willy-nilly," as Representative J. D. Hayworth, Republican of Arizona, recently put it (though "willy-willy" probably comes closer to what he had in mind).

Listening to arguments like those can make you sympathize with legislators in Massachusetts and elsewhere who are trying to find a way to confer the rights without the title, even if "civil union" ultimately comes down to marriage with an asterisk. Whether their reservations are personal or political, they're not pretending that nothing more than "mere semantics" is at stake.

In the end, though, the meaning of *marriage* will be determined by the way ordinary people use the word, not the edicts of courts or legislatures. And popular usage can be surprisingly adaptable—as attitudes evolve, it has few qualms about modifying the traditional definitions of words, however sanctified they seem at the time.

Take *couple*. The latest edition of the *Oxford English Dictionary* still defines the word as "A man and woman united by love or marriage." And the phrase "homosexual couple" didn't appear in *The New York Times* in 1967, with "gay couple" making its *Times* debut in the following year in a well-intended *Sunday Magazine* article called "Civil Rights and the Homosexual." (The writer urged tolerance of homosexuality "either as an emotional disorder or an unalterable sexual deviation," but stressed that "scholars of homosexual culture cannot foresee any equivalent of marriage for homosexuals.") Yet just a few decades later, reservations about referring to "gay couples" seem as quaint as that phrase "the homosexual," which reduced a group to a uniform anthropological type.

The meaning of *family* has been changing, too. The third edition of the *American Heritage Dictionary*, published in 1992, defines the word as "a fundamental social group typically consisting of a man and woman and their offspring." But when the fourth edition came out in 2000, the last part of the definition was altered to "typically consisting of one or two parents and their children." The new wording is descriptive, not prescriptive. Families today don't strike us as "atypical" simply because they don't conform to the domestic configuration of *Father Knows Best*.

The definition of *marriage* is becoming more inclusive, as well. A new Canadian edition of the OED defines the word as "the legal or religious union of two people." (While the editors of the OED are at it, you hope they'll revisit their definition of *couple*—and for that matter, of *love* in the romantic sense, which currently runs, "That feeling of attachment which is based upon difference of sex.")

True, the resistance to changing the meaning of *marriage* runs deeper than with other words. But usage rarely stands on principle. As more same-sex couples are married in religious or civil ceremonies, sentences like "Jane and June have been married for 15 years" are bound to become part of the linguistic wallpaper of the media in the same way "gay couple" has. Whom God has joined together, *People* magazine is not about to put asunder.

At that point, we can talk about a genuine change in semantics—though there certainly won't be anything "mere" about it. And sooner or later, the legal forms will inevitably follow suit. As William Hazlitt wrote in 1830: "Laws and institutions are positive things" (that is to say, formally established arrangements) "while opinions and sentiments are variable; and it is in conforming the stubbornness and perversity of the former to the freedom and boldness of the latter, that the harmony and beauty of the social order consists."

Obscenity Rap

Every age swears differently from the last one—it's as if we have to up the ante every generation or so. As Jonathan Swift wrote:

> . . . now-a-days Men change their Oaths
> As often as they change their Cloaths.

Hence the problems faced by the writers of historical fictions nowadays. If you have your characters use historically accurate swearwords, they're apt to sound no more offensive than your grandmother in a mild snit. The only way to convey the potency of the characters' oaths is to have them use modern swearwords, even if they're anachronistic.

That's the approach taken by the HBO series *Deadwood*, set in a South Dakota mining camp in the 1870s. As a lot of people have noted, the show is positively swilling in obscenity—the characters use *fuck* and *fucking* with a frequency that would make Tony Soprano blush.

But *fuck* wasn't actually a swearword back then. It was indecent, of course, but people only used it for the sexual act itself. Whereas swearwords are the ones that become detached from their literal meanings and float free as mere intensifiers. Swearing isn't using *fucking* when you're referring to sex, it's using it when you're talking about the weather.

In fact when you look up *fuck* in Jonathan Lighter's magisterial *Dictionary of American Slang*, you discover that the all-purpose insult *fuck you* was a turn-of-the-twentieth-century creation, and *go fuck yourself* isn't attested until 1920. *Fucked up* and *Don't fuck with me* didn't show up till around the time of the Second World War. And while people may have been emphasizing nouns with *fucking* from the 1890s, it wasn't until well into the twentieth century that you heard things like "She fucking well better tell me" or "Get the fuck out of here," both *Deadwood* favorites.

The same holds for most of the other obscene words that you hear on *Deadwood*. Back in the 19th century, people used *asshole* to refer to a bodily orifice, but it was only in the 1920s that anybody thought to apply the words to a despicable person. And it was around the same time that the new word "motherfucker" was coined with roughly the same meaning.

True, it isn't always easy to tell exactly when these uses of obscene words came into general use—they're not the sorts of items you run into in Henry James. But actually there are plenty of nineteenth-century examples of *fuck* being used in a literal way in letters, pornographic novels, and slang dictionaries, and other swearwords show up pretty frequently as well. And if *fuck* and the rest had been used in an extended way as swearwords, it's a safe bet those uses would have showed up in the same kinds of sources.

The swearwords those *Deadwood* characters would actually have used had religious overtones rather than sexual or scatological ones. They would have peppered their speech with *goddamn*, *Jesus*, and particularly *hell*, a word that nineteenth-century Ameri-

cans were famous for using with a dazzling virtuosity—"a hell of
a drink," "What in hell did that mean?," "hell to pay," "The hell
you will," "hell-bent," "Hell, yes," "like a bat out of hell," "hell's
bells," and countless others.

Back then, those oaths were strong enough to spawn a whole
vocabulary of the substitutes that H. L. Mencken called "denatur-
ized profanities"—*darn, doggone, dadburned, tarnation, goldarn, gee-
whiz, all-fired*, and the like. (It's only in the 1920s that you start
running into substitutes for *fucking* like *freaking* or *effing*—another
sign that it wasn't used as a swearword before then.) But if you
put words like *goldarn* into the mouths of the characters on *Deadwood*, they'd all wind up sounding like Yosemite Sam.

One reason for the shift is that old-fashioned blasphemy didn't
have the same illicit thrill for a secular age. When I was a kid I
was always a little puzzled about the commandment about taking the Lord's name in vain. Not that I didn't know better than to
say *goddamn* at the dinner table. But when people listed the Ten
Commandments, it was hard to see why the profanity rap should
get a higher billing than murder, theft, or perjury.

That change in attitudes is what drove World War I dough-
boys into the bedroom and bathroom looking for new bound-
aries to trespass. That shift was more than a simple change of
fashion. The old profanity was a matter of irreverence—using
respectable words in disrespectful contexts. The new obscenity is
the opposite of that. It's a kind of linguistic slumming, where we
bring unclean words into the rooms at the front of the house.
The taboo against profanity comes from on high; the taboo
against obscenity comes from within.

The shift had a lot to do with the great leveling of swearing
over the past century. The Victorians liked to think of swearing as

a vice endemic to men of the lower orders—one swore "like a trooper," or "like a sailor." Nowadays swearing isn't a mark of any particular class or gender; the words are dirty little secrets we can all draw on when we find ourselves in an angry or aggressive mood. You don't find many people nowadays who will tell you that they never swear—and if they do, they're most likely bragging about their even temper, not their gentility or their piety.

The new rituals of swearing have altered the hypocrisy that surrounds the practice, too. Time was that swearwords were completely absent from public discourse, and genteel people could go through their lives pretending they didn't exist. Nowadays, it's more a question of maintaining an official sanctimony in designated public forums.

You can use *fuck* in *The New Yorker* but not in *The New York Times*. Bill Maher can say *fuck* on HBO but not on ABC, and Jon Stewart can say it on the Comedy Channel, but with the understanding it will be bleeped. Steven Sondheim can use *shit* in a song when *Sweeney Todd* plays in theaters (though actually that one is an anachronism, too), but public radio shows are apt to have qualms about playing the song over the air, particularly in the current climate. As one public radio producer put it recently, "This isn't just about seven words anymore."

Of course we have to draw a line somewhere, if swearing is going to have any transgressive force at all. The wonder is that people can still defend distinctions like those with a keen moral fervor, even in an age when more than 90 percent of Americans pay for some form of subscription TV. The Victorians would have had a hard time understanding how our sense of outrage about swearing could fluctuate according to where we are on the dial.

Propaganda in Drag

Nobody blinks an eye these days when advertisers ape news-show formats in TV infomercials. So the Department of Health and Human Services must have been surprised when the General Accounting Office announced in February of 2004 that they'd be investigating the department's use of the same techniques to promote the Bush Administration's prescription-drug bill. The department sent out a video news release to extol the virtues of the bill, complete with fake reporters and a shot of President Bush receiving a standing ovation as he signed the bill.

On Comedy Central's *Daily Show*, one of John Stewart's mock-correspondents described that kind of bogus newscast as "infoganda," and worried that it might drive genuine fake newscasts like Stewart's off the air. And in *The New York Times*, Frank Rich extended *infoganda* to the range of ploys the administration has used to spin news coverage, from the manipulation of the Jessica Lynch story, the "Mission Accomplished" photo op aboard the USS *Abraham Lincoln,* and the editorial direction it offered to Showtime's docudrama *D.C, 9/11* to the TV blitz by Condoleezza Rice and others aimed at discrediting Richard Clarke.

As it happens, *infoganda* has been kicking around for a

Fresh Air commentary, April 2, 2004

while—it first appeared in the press during the Gulf War of 1991 as a description of the reports and footage that the Pentagon was furnishing to journalists. But the word may very well have been independently coined on several occasions. It's a natural for this sort of thing—it fits the pattern of those spliced-together port-manteau words like *infotainment* and *docudrama*. Names like those are the linguistic version of *Junkyard Wars*—there's nothing new under the sun, apart from what you can cobble together from the stuff that's lying around the shop.

What's curious about *infoganda* is that anyone would feel the need for a new word to describe those government-produced news videos. There was a time when that territory would have been adequately covered by *propaganda*, a genre that has always worked best in drag.

Propaganda was originally coined by the Jesuits in the seven-teenth century as the name of the Vatican committee charged with propagating the faith, but it didn't become part of the every-day vocabulary until the time of the First World War, when the British and Germans began to use the new techniques of mass advertising and public relations to rouse popular support for their cause. Looking back on the period a few decades later, the jour-nalist Will Irwin observed: "Before 1914, 'propaganda' belonged only to literate vocabularies and possessed a reputable, dignified meaning... Two years later the word had come into the vocabu-lary of peasants and ditchdiggers and had begun to acquire its miasmic aura."

Americans got into this game when the country entered the war in 1917. President Wilson set up the Committee on Public Information, modeled on the British Department of Information. It became known as the Creel Committee after its chairman, the journalist George Creel. The committee churned out posters, pamphlets and press releases, and enlisted 75,000 people to serve as "four minute men," who gave short prepared speeches and lantern-slide shows at theaters and public gatherings, urging people to enlist or buy liberty bonds.

Most of that material was pretty purple stuff, laced with phrases like "bombs or bondage" and "If you don't come across, the Kaiser will." But Creel denied that the committee was trafficking in propaganda, a word he associated with "deceit and corruption." "Our effort," he said, "was educational and informative throughout. No other argument was needed than the simple, straightforward presentation of facts."

As time went on, public wariness turned *propaganda* into an orphan word that no one would own up to—in 1939, a poll showed 40 percent of Americans blamed propaganda for the US entry into the First World War. In that environment, propagandists took greater pains to disguise their product. In 1938, one New York editor objected to the deluge of phony press releases from the "news services" that had been set up by foreign governments to win favorable coverage. He warned that they threatened to break down the line of demarcation between news and propaganda, particularly if papers began to rely on them to fill their pages.

But of course that was exactly the point of the exercise. By then it was clear that propaganda was most effective when it masqueraded as objective news. In 1941, when FDR wanted to drum up support for extending the draft and increasing American aid to the British war effort, he established an Office of Facts and Figures, headed by Archibald MacLeish. Some isolationist senators accused the administration of trying to set up a centralized propaganda bureau, but New York's mayor Fiorello LaGuardia, who had been an advocate of the program, reassured the public that "the office is not a propaganda agency. . . We don't believe in this country in artificially stimulated, high-pressure, doctored nonsense." Even so, in a private memo to Roosevelt, LaGuardia admitted that the agency's goal was to provide the public with what he called "sugar coated, colored, ornamental matter, otherwise known as 'bunk.'"

By 1942, the Office of Facts and Figures had been absorbed into the Office of War Information, which was also encouraging Hollywood to make movies that roused patriotic sentiments. In the words of the agency's director, the journalist Elmer Davis: "The easiest way to inject a propaganda idea into most men's minds is to let it go in through the medium of an entertainment picture."

Ultimately, the American propagandists' greatest victory was to discredit the word *propaganda* itself. By the time of the Cold War, *propaganda* only referred to what the other side said—and said crudely, at that. The word conjured up the bombast and strident language of the Soviets, not the soft-sell productions of our side. Propaganda programs were the ones with the Red Army Chorus in the background, not Stan Kenton.

So it isn't surprising that the use of *propaganda* continued to decline with détente, the end of the Vietnam war, and then the fall of Communism. Over the past five years, the word has been only a tenth as common in the press as it was in its Cold War heyday. That may be why people felt the need to coin *infoganda* to describe the fake news shows and contrived photo ops that are designed to blend seamlessly into the media background.

Still, while there may be nothing new about these techniques, the current administration has exploited them more deftly than anyone since Roosevelt's day. And they've found a fertile ground for their plantings in the modern media setting, which already blurs the lines between journalism and advocacy and reality and fiction.

As a Department of Health and Human Services spokesman said in defending the fake news spot about the prescription drug bill, "Anyone who has questions about this practice needs to do some research on modern public information tools." It's hard to argue with that. In a world of infomercials, advertorials, and docudramas, what's one more imposture?

Power to the People

"Shop like a populist," wrote a columnist in the *St. Petersburg Times* not long ago, recommending a local store that specializes in "quirky collectibles" like old soap boxes and bowling pins.

That's what the *pop* of *populist* has come to, a century after the disappearance of the Populists, or People's Party, who were a powerful political force in the 1890s. The original Populists advocated restrictions on corporate power, the direct election of United States senators, an eight-hour day, and a graduated income tax—proposals that led critics to call them "wild-eyed, rattle-brained fanatics."

Within a few years, though, the party had fallen apart, and over the first half of the twentieth century, "populist" became an increasingly quaint and old-fashioned word, used mostly to disparage demagogues like Louisiana's governor Huey P. Long. It was only in the 1960s that a new generation of politicians began to reclaim the label. In 1972, C. Vann Woodward wrote an article in *The New York Times Magazine* called "The Ghost of Populism Walks Again," marveling at the way the label was turning up in "improbable and unaccustomed quarters." It was laid claim to not just by the New Left but by many on the right, who divested it of the awkward connotations of class struggle that had alarmed their own ideological ancestors.

Over the past two decades, *populism* has been 15 times as common in the press as it was during the Eisenhower years. But now it can refer not just to those who speak for the downtrodden, but to anyone or anything whose appeal seems down home, down to earth, or down market. In recent press articles, I've seen the word applied to Michael Moore, John Edwards, Garth Brooks, Steven Spielberg, Arnold Schwarzenegger, Fox News, Burger King, Donald Trump, Muktada al-Sadr, the Google IPO, and Oscar de la Renta's new mid-price fashion line.

Nowadays populism sometimes comes down to no more than what mode of locomotion you favor. In *Boston Magazine*, Jon Keller speaks of John Kerry's difficulty in "convincing southern NASCAR dads and Wal-Mart moms of the populist empathy of a windsurfing New England multimillionaire." *National Review*'s Jay Nordlinger writes that "President Bush is engaged in a little populist campaigning himself today—he's going to Indiana and Michigan, for a bus tour."

Sometimes, in fact, the word doesn't seem to mean much more than "popular." "I know that's the populist view to say those things," said Rep. Porter Goss on CNBC after Sen. Carl Levin suggested that American credibility had suffered in the wake of intelligence failures.

Along the way, *populism* has lost not just its capital letter, but its connection to the sense of "the people" that the name was derived from. That's "the people," not as the populace or the citizenry, but as what William Jennings Bryan described as the "unnumbered throng" who were oppressed by the corporations, the money interests and the trusts, "aggregated wealth and capital, imperious, arrogant, compassionless."

Those antagonisms sound creaky now, like "the people" itself. The "money interest" has yielded to "the elite," as populism has become a matter of "values," rather than class. "What divides America is authenticity, not something hard or ugly like economics," as Thomas Frank suggests in *What's the Matter With Kansas?*, a look at how the new populism has captured the imagination of the state that gave birth to the old one.

True, "the people" still exerts a nostalgic hold on some. When the Republicans descended on New York City for their convention, two New Yorkers distributed a "People's Guide to the Republican Convention," a title that made it clear that the guide was compiled for the benefit of protesters, not delegates. And Vice President Al Gore used the phrase in his acceptance speech at the Democratic convention of 2000: "They're for the powerful. We're for the people."

But "the people" were absent from the speeches at both the Democratic and Republican conventions, except when accompanied by minders like "ordinary," "hard-working," or "good." Nowadays, "power to the people" is a slogan used by both Microsoft and IBM. And "man of the people" invariably has a sarcastic inflection. The *Boston Herald* styled the 2004 Democratic presidential candidate as "Man of the People Kerry." On CNN's "Capital Gang," Mark Shields wondered how "that populist man of the people, George W. Bush," would deal with the New York firefighters who had been waiting for a raise since September 11, 2001.

The sarcasm usually reflects skepticism about the candidates' authenticity, rather than about their policies. ("He is not a man of the people, this French-speaking windsurfer," said Richard Reeves of Senator Kerry—transportation again.) Populism used to be a matter of speaking for the people; now it's a matter of speaking like them—dropping your g's, strategically mispronouncing *nuclear*, and peppering your speeches with references to motor sports.

The old-style populists made no concessions to popular style. The "Cross of Gold" speech that secured Bryan the presidential nomination at the Democratic convention of 1896 (and a place at the head of the Populist ticket, as well) is remembered today for its stirring peroration: "You shall not press down upon the brow of labor this crown of thorns; you shall not crucify mankind upon a cross of gold." But the speech was also studded with allusions to Cicero, Napoleon, Jefferson, and Peter the Hermit, and it included a 1200-word disquisition on bimetallism and monetary policy that began:

> Let me remind you that there is no intention of affecting those contracts which, according to present laws, are made payable in gold, but if he means to say that we cannot change our monetary system without protecting those who have loaned money before the change was made, I desire to ask him where, in law or in morals, he can find justification for not protecting the debtors when the act of 1873 was passed, if he now insists that we must protect the creditors...

And so on for another four or five paragraphs of redoubtably fustian syntax. The average sentence in Bryan's speech was 104 words long; the average sentence in George W. Bush's 2000 acceptance speech was less than 15 words long.

Rhetoric changes with the times, of course. But even if you simplified Bryan's diction and syntax and pruned the florid turns of phrase, the speech wouldn't come off now as "populist," but as artificial, ponderous, and more than a little wonky. Yet at the time, it kept audiences rapt. What seems most remote about that bygone age is the image of thousands of farmers, shopkeepers and small-town mechanics flocking to railroad depots to hear their champion repeat the "Cross of Gold" speech as he campaigned across the West in the summer of 1896, the scene Vachel Lindsay described in his poem "Bryan, Bryan, Bryan, Bryan":

> . . . the town was all one spreading wing of bunting, plumes,
> and sunshine,
> > Every rag and flag, and Bryan picture sold,
> > When the rigs in many a dusty line
> > Jammed our streets at noon,
> > And joined the wild parade against the power of gold.

Were the people merely more patient listeners back then, or have politicians lost the knack of speaking to them without condescending?

Geezers, Gerries, and Golden Agers

I was talking to the 20-something son of a friend of mine in New York about his vacation plans. "I'm going to grandma's place in Florida to spend a week with the gerries," he said. It took me a moment to realize that the word was a truncation of "geriatric." It's a useful item for sorting out the generations—if you still think *gerry* refers to Germans, then it may very well refer to you.

It's too soon to tell whether *gerry* will catch on. But it's normal for the generation that's coming of age to coin names for the one that's passing from center stage, not just in its slang, but in its official vocabulary as well. Recently, the Progressive Policy Institute held a panel to promote its proposal for a Boomer Corps, a national service program for older Americans. According to the PPI's Mark Magee, the name was chosen to suggest a range of activities broader than those traditionally associated with retirees. But some people have worried that *boomer* might acquire more derogatory connotations as people over 65 come to constitute a quarter of the population, particularly if it's perceived that they're getting a better deal on Social Security than younger people are.

It wouldn't be the first time that words for old people went from positive to disparaging. In the eighteenth century, *gaffer* was a term of respect for old people, most likely derived from *godfather*, and *fogy* was simply a word for a veteran; by the beginning of the nineteenth century both had become derisive words. Around the same time, *codger*, *old guard* and *superannuated* acquired pejorative senses, joined later in the century by new disparagements like *fuddy-duddy*, *coot* and *geezer*.

The historian David Hackett Fischer argued in *Growing Old in America* that those shifts reflected a dramatic change in society, as deference to the old was replaced by contempt and neglect. The difference is symbolized by a shift from the age-becoming fashions of the eighteenth century to the youthful ones of the early nineteenth century: powdered wigs and loose, full-cut coats and gowns yielded to diaphanous dresses for women and to toupees, tight trousers, and high collars for men. And while historians are divided on whether the condition of the old really declined in that period, it's clear that people were referring to old people more irreverently.

Age-disparaging words are the natural by-product of a cult of youth, so it's not surprising that so many of them appeared in the Boomer Age, whose fashions and language are a constant reminder of what a drag it is getting old. Since the 1950s, the language has added *dinosaur*, *fossil*, *blue-hair*, *cotton-top*, *gerry*, and *trog*, as well as flip terms for parents like *rents* and *p's*. Gays speak of trolls, who hang out in bars called wrinkle rooms. And that's not to mention British imports like *wrinkly*, *crinkly*, and *crumbly*, which taken together sound like a law firm out of *Bleak House*.

The circumlocutions and euphemisms people use when speaking of the aged are equally revealing. The Victorians coined *of a mature age* and *70 years young*, a turn of phrase first credited to Oliver Wendell Holmes. The twentieth century brought *senior*

citizen, golden ager and *Third Age*. (The last is supposed to desig-
nate the productive years between retirement and dependency,
but it has been suffering from bracket creep at the upper end—
most people seem to find three ages quite enough and are in no
hurry to enter a fourth.) And the comparative *older* has been re-
deployed as an absolute term—when somebody talks about
"older Americans" nowadays, we're no longer tempted to ask,
"Older than whom?"

Granted, some of those phrases reflect a new perception of
age as an important social issue. However fulsome *senior citizen*
may sound, it's the first term to acknowledge the old as a political
constituency. But apart from the useful new use of "older" and
the ironic "senior moment," most of these euphemisms are too
forced for everyday conversation. And even in political and business contexts, they're often replaced with even more oblique
phraseology. Banks have abandoned "senior accounts" for "Classic checking" or "Renaissance checking," and the airlines' programs for older fliers go by names like "AActive American
Traveler," "Young at Heart," and "Silver Wings Travel Club."
Euphemism is like waxing a floor—you have to keep reapplying
new coats as the old ones yellow.

The condescension of our euphemisms and the impertinence
of our slang both testify to our discomfort about confronting the
facts of age head-on. As G. K. Chesterton remarked 80 years ago
in his essay "The Prudery of Slang":

> "There was a time when it was customary to call a father a
> father.... Now, it appears to be considered a mark of
> advanced intelligence to call your father a bean or a scream.
> It is obvious to me that calling the old gentleman 'father' is

facing the facts of nature. It is also obvious that calling him 'bean' is merely weaving a graceful fairy tale to cover the facts of nature."

True, these facts of nature leave every Western society a bit ill at ease. The British, French and Germans talk about the old with the same mix of irreverence and euphemism as Americans. But only the United States makes youth an essential feature of its national self-conception. As C. Vann Woodward once put it, we see ourselves as "the eternal Peter Pan among nations," even if by world standards we're at best early-fall chickens.

The youthfulness of our generational language may make it even harder for us baby boomers to come to terms with our lengthening demographic shadow. Linguistically, though, we'll have to reap what we have sown. As Chesterton said of the young people of his own age, "As they have no defense against their fathers except a new fashion, they will have no defense against their sons except an old fashion."

[Word Index]

[Subject Index]

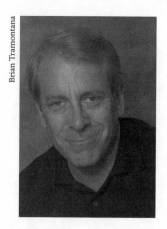

Brian Tramontana

ABOUT THE AUTHOR

GEOFFREY NUNBERG is a senior researcher at the Center for
the Study of Language and Information at Stanford University
and Consulting Full Professor of Linguistics at Stanford University. He is a chair of the Usage Panel of the *American Heritage
Dictionary*. He does a regular language feature on NPR's *Fresh
Air* and writes regular features about language and topical issues
for the Sunday *New York Times* "Week in Review."